THE UNIVERSAL 12-STEP PROGRAM

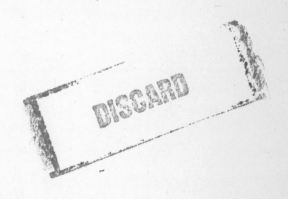

THE UNIVERSAL
12-Step
PROGRAM

How to Overcome Any Addiction and Win!

Kenneth Peiser, Ph.D.
and
Martin Sandry, Ph.D.

Adams Media Corporation
Holbrook, Massachusetts

Published by
Adams Media Corporation
260 Center Street, Holbrook, MA 02343

ISBN: 1-58062-213-5

Printed in the United States of America
J I H G F E D C B A

Library of Congress Cataloging-in-Publication Data
Peiser, Kenneth.
The universal 12-step program : how to overcome any addiction
and win! / by Kenneth Peiser, and Martin Sandry.
p. cm.
Includes bibliographical references.
ISBN 1-58062-213-5
1. Twelve-step programs. 2. Recovering addicts. 3. Addicts–Rehabilitation.
I. Sandry, Martin. II. Title. III. Title: Universal twelve-step program.
HV4998.P45   1999
616.86'03–dc21   99-15776
CIP

This publication is designed to provide accurate and authoritative information with
regard to the subject matter covered. It is sold with the understanding that the
publisher is not engaged in rendering legal, accounting, or other professional
advice. If legal advice or other expert assistance is required, the services of a
competent professional person should be sought.

— From a Declaration of Principles jointly adopted by a Committee of the
American Bar Association and a Committee of Publishers and Associations

This book is available at quantity discounts for bulk purchases.
For information, call 1-800-872-5627.

Visit our home page at http://www.adamsmedia.com

The authors dedicate this book to Nancy Sandry, whose constant encouragement and loving prodding not only enabled but almost forced this work to be written. We also want to thank her for her infinite patience, especially when her landscape was littered with notes and piles of papers, and for planning many of her life events around our writing schedules, all with indefinite beginning and ending times. We both love her very much.

Contents

Foreword

When I first created Rational Emotive Therapy (RET) in January 1955, I used it with my clients who had all kinds of emotional problems, including addiction. I later saw that it is more helpful for almost any addiction than any other form of psychotherapy, including the cognitive-behavior therapies that began to follow RET principles and practices in the 1960s. Jack Trimpey, an RET practitioner for the last quarter of a century, also noted its advantages in regard to his own addiction; wrote *Rational Recovery: The Small Book* in 1989; and began an alternative group to Alcoholics Anonymous, Rational Recovery, at the same time. Rational Recovery now has hundreds of self-help groups for problem drinkers and other addicts in the United States and many foreign countries.

Marty Sandry and Ken Peiser also began to practice RET in the 1960s and soon used it extensively with problem drinkers and other addicts. This book beautifully summarizes their work in this field and very clearly applies the main principles of Rational Emotive Therapy to recovery. As is usual in RET, their book shows how you, the reader, can not only get help from working with a psychotherapist but also apply RET successfully on your own. This form of therapy has sparked many popular self-help books, including my own *New Guide to Rational Living* and *How to Stubbornly Refuse to Make Yourself Miserable About Anything,—Yes, Anything!*, and Marty and Ken's book is one of the best. It is exceptionally hardheaded, precise, and down to earth and includes many practical exercises that you can use on your own.

As I have explained at length in my books *Rational Emotive Therapy With Alcoholics and Substance Abusers* and *When AA Doesn't Work For You: Rational Steps to Quitting Alcohol*, most problem drinkers and other addicts first have general emotional problems—especially severe anxiety and depression—and then resort to some addiction to cover up these problems and to temporarily allay them. Therefore, they usually create severe self-downing as well as low frustration tolerance, which serve to drive them to addiction and also to damn themselves for their addiction and thereby make it worse.

This book, like those of Jack Trimpey, myself, and other RET practitioners, shows you how to tackle both your general emotional disturbances and your specific addiction problems. If you carefully heed and use its messages you won't guarantee yourself good mental health and freedom from addiction, but you will most probably greatly increase your chances of acquiring both these valuable behaviors.

Albert Ellis, Ph.D., President
Albert Ellis Institute
45 East 65th Street
New York, NY 10021-6593

Preface

Doctors Ken Peiser and Martin Sandry developed the ideas presented in this book while working with patients of LIFELINE, Ltd. LIFELINE, Ltd., is a scientifically oriented chemical dependency center where I have been the medical director since its inception in 1984. Their concept of the chain of conditioned addictive reactions came from patients' direct descriptions of their experiences. It is a unique, coherent explanation of the addiction process and an important contribution to the addictions field. The revised twelve steps opens a door for those to whom this process was previously inaccessible. The revised steps clarify, even for traditional twelve-step devotees, the psychological meaning and the significance of the twelve steps.

The many cognitive-behavioral exercises engage patients in actively working on their own recovery in a structured way instead of just listening to the experiences of others and sharing their own. They incorporate many scientifically validated contemporary therapeutic concepts and practices. Given the recent advent of managed care—which, in most cases has greatly shortened the availability and length of in-patient treatment—this book can serve as a partial substitute for some of the work and education that we used to be able to do in the more protective in-patient environment. Anyone who works through the text and conscientiously does the exercises prescribed throughout this book has a high probability of recovering from an addiction or habit of choice, whether it is a chemical, a behavioral, or an emotional addiction, or any combination thereof.

Sheldon S. Greenberg, M.D.

Acknowledgments

We would like to acknowledge the contributions of many people who have given us the information, wisdom, and direction that we hope are exemplified in this book. We cannot come close, in just a page or two, to doing so, but here are some examples.

Dr. Albert Ellis, probably the world's most renowned psychotherapist in the past few decades, taught us, personally, the theory and practice of Rational Emotive Behavior Therapy. Having both been trained in nondirective (client-centered) therapy when we met Al in 1966, we were astonished to find that it was okay to answer a client's questions, to give commonsense advice, to tell the client that his or her thinking was wrong, and to vigorously encourage clients to change their errant/dysfunctional ways. While all of this might seem, these days, to be commonplace or obviously good clinical practice, back in those days it was condemned by most extant schools of psychotherapeutic thought. Today, some thirty-plus years later, most mental health specialists, except the strict psychopharmacologists, want to be considered as doing cognitive behavioral therapy.

Next we must recognize, perhaps even more than Albert Ellis or any other "experts," the three thousand or so addicted persons whom we have had the privilege to know, care for, and treat at eight different facilities as well as in our private practices.

Others have been important to the shaping of this work. Blair Anton worked with us on the formulation of the chain of addictive conditioned reactions and has taught it to addicts for the past six years. Mary Larsen, one of our program directors at LIFELINE, Ltd., answered every problem we brought to her with, "Fix it." Mary also taught us a great lesson by hanging a sign above her desk that says, "Addicts Lie." This is something that patients and staff don't like to hear, but it sure is true. Sheryl Smith, as another one of our LIFE-LINE program directors, provided us the time to formulate these ideas. Sheldon Greenberg, M.D., taught us almost all we know about psychotropic medications—their limitations and potentials.

Finally, we wish to thank Jere Calmes, who gave us the opportunity to publish this work, and Anne Weaver, our editor, who repeatedly told us that things were going well.

None of these people who have contributed to this book necessarily accept or are responsible for all of the views that we have expressed herein.

Introduction

What Are Addictive Behaviors?

Addictive behaviors are those behaviors that have gotten out of control. We are all familiar with alcoholism, drug addiction, and overeating to the point of obesity, as well as other habits. There are many other examples of addiction, including addictions to throwing up after eating, to sex, to shopping, to tobacco, to television watching, and even to emotional states such as anger, self-pity, or fear of other people (rejection). If we include workaholism and addictions to sports or exercise, to destructive relationships, to computers, to Net surfing, and to chat rooms, the chances are that virtually everyone has some behavior that has gotten out of control. A behavior is out of control when there is a struggle between what we know makes sense for us and what we actually do.

If there are things that you overdo that you have tried to limit, you may be addicted. Later in this book you will be asked to rate yourself on a number of behaviors in order to determine which of those, for you, are addictive problems. If you are in the grip of such problems, you might already recognize the difficulty in overcoming them.

It is also possible, however, that you have habits that you do not see as problems but that others think are problems for you. One of the main difficulties in overcoming an addiction is recognizing that you are, in fact, addicted—that you have actually lost control over your behavior. Frequently, those of you who are dependent on some substance or behavior sincerely believe that you would have no problem stopping the behavior. Many people very often have, in fact, tried to stop the behavior many times without success. Sometimes, they have temporarily stopped the behavior, only to relapse into the old behavior pattern once again. Most people who have tried to stop drinking, lose weight, stop smoking, give up drugs, stop having inappropriate sex, or stop gambling or overspending have experienced this problem of relapse.

What Does Recovery Mean?

Recovery means running your life in such a fashion as not to relapse *and still be happy*. As you will see in the following history of recovery programs, the precise meaning of "recovery" and the means to go about it differ from one program to another. A program of recovery is simply a set of guidelines as to how to live your life without being dependent upon some substance or behavior in order to feel happy and to feel fulfilled. Different recovery programs may define relapse differently. Some will say that *any* indulgence in the uncontrolled behavior is relapse. Others will say that some "slips" do not really constitute a relapse. Finally, some will even say that controlled indulgence is the goal, and as long as the use of the substance or indulgence in the addictive behavior is controlled, there is no relapse.

All of the twelve-step programs dedicated to overcoming chemical dependencies insist upon total abstinence from the substance of choice as well as all other mood- or mind-altering drugs except, sometimes, prescribed psychotropic medications. Sex Anonymous and Overeaters Anonymous, as well as some other programs, advocate limited or controlled indulgence for obvious reasons. Initially, abstinence from all addictions was not a consideration, since Alcoholics

Anonymous (AA) originally thought little about nicotine and caffeine dependencies. The typical AA meeting involves lots of smoking and coffee drinking even today.

It was Narcotics Anonymous (NA) that first called for abstinence from all drugs. At first, heroin addicts were allowed to drink. Later, because many heroin addicts gave up heroin only to switch to alcohol addiction, NA prescribed total abstinence. Alcoholics Anonymous eventually adopted this position, although neither organization stresses giving up caffeine, nicotine, overeating, or any of the behavioral addictions. But NA and AA strongly discourage the psychiatric use of tranquilizers and antidepressants, although this prohibition is slowly changing for some groups. There is thus a wide range, even within the "orthodox" twelve-step programs, of what is or is not considered "recovery."

The position we take here is the nondogmatic one that *you* have to define recovery for yourself. If you decide that you want to control your use, and can reliably do so, more power to you! If you decide to use some substances but abstain from others, that is *your* choice. Most addicted persons will probably find out that total abstinence is, in the long run, the easiest way to prevent relapse. Whatever your goal, partial or total abstinence, we believe that this program can help—with no dogma, and with or without God, religion, or spirituality.

A Brief History of Recovery Programs

There were a number of early attempts to help alcoholics but for various reasons these mostly faded out. There are currently several approaches to helping people give up self-destructive behaviors to which they are addicted. The most famous of these is Alcoholics Anonymous, begun in 1935 by a small group of people whom the medical/psychiatric community could not help. Bill Wilson and Dr.

Bob, the primary founders of AA, developed a program of twelve guidelines (steps) to recovery from alcoholism. The steps were formulated in answer to the question "How did you do it?" (stop drinking), and are thus stated in the sequential order that Bill and Dr. Bob themselves used, after many failed attempts, to succeed in attaining their goal of sobriety. The steps, therefore, were written in terms of "We did this; then we did that." The program involved alcoholics banding together in groups that looked to faith in a divine spiritual force to help them stop drinking. By 1939, AA had grown to about one hundred recovering alcoholics. They published a retrospective account of their recovery process in order to share their recovery experiences with other alcoholics. The name of the book is *Alcoholics Anonymous*, but is usually referred to as the *Big Book*.

This program then became incorporated by drug addicts (NA, which mostly involved opiate addicts), then later by cocaine addicts (CA), and eventually by overeaters (OA), gamblers (GA), sex addicts (SA), nicotine addicts, and even emotionally disturbed persons (EA) as a way to recovery. The "anonymous" part refers to the fact that those people who wanted this kind of help did not want to publicly acknowledge that they had an addictive problem. At first, they refused to meet in any room lower than the second floor, in case someone they knew walked by and recognized them through the window. The original concept included the idea that the group was so special and anonymous a new member could only enter the ranks of the recovering by being "sponsored" into the group by someone who knew that the alcoholic could keep the group and his or her membership in the group a secret from outsiders. The concept of *sponsorship* was thus born, and it continues, though in another sense, in the Anonymous groups today. Later, anonymity became an exercise in humility in order to challenge the tendency to grandstand or brag about being a recovering person.

However, many addicts do not—or cannot—accept the fundamental idea of the original AA system that reliance on *spirituality* or a "Higher Power" is the sole answer to recovery from addiction. For this reason, groups such as Atheists and Agnostics Alcoholics Anonymous (AAAA), Rational Recovery Systems (RR), Secular Organizations for Sobriety (SOS), and Self Management and Recovery Training (SMART) were originated.

Rational Approaches to Recovery

The RR program, founded by Jack and Lois Trimpey, was originally based upon the ABC Theory of Rational Emotive Behavior Therapy (REBT), as is the program presented here. A major difference between RR and our program is that we recognize the fact that AA, NA, CA, and other "A" (Anonymous) group programs have established a record of helping people recover and resist relapse. RR, in denying any validity to the twelve-step program, throws the baby out with the bath water because there are numerous aspects of the twelve-step program that are helpful.

We have attempted to extract those psychologically correct parts of the "A" program(s) that make them work—the psychological essence that serves as the underpinning that influences people to change their behavior patterns and find happiness. To that program we added the most research-proven, effective Rational Emotive/cognitive-behavioral methods of psychological change, which emphasize changing thoughts and actions in order to bring feelings and behaviors into a more appropriate adjustment to reality.

Throughout this book we shall attempt to teach you about the traditional "A" approach, so that in the absence of, or in spite of, the availability of RR or SOS groups in your area, you can still take advantage of the many "A" groups in your area in order to experience the feeling of support provided by the fellowship and sponsorship aspects of these programs. The Glossary of Recovery Terms at the end of this book explains many of the phrases you'll hear over and over again in the traditional "A" groups.

If you do have RR or SOS groups in your area, we recommend that you attend them! We further recommend, if you can afford it, that your sponsor be a Rational Emotive Behavior therapist who is familiar with recovery programs; note that not all REBT therapists are. In fact, we recommend attending a variety of recovery groups so that you can broaden your experience and determine which is your particular "cup of tea." Some recovering persons have expressed interest in developing self-help groups based upon this Rational Emotive recovery program. By the time you read this, one or more such groups might be available in your area. These groups would welcome members of any other self-help groups, regardless of the nature of the problem addressed by those groups and regardless of their philosophy.

Again, this book is intended to help those of all religious or areligious philosophies. By the time you get through it, you will be able to profit from RR, SOS, AA, NA, CA, and the other "A" groups whether you do or do not believe in a sentient God or consider yourself a religious or spiritual person. What *is* essential for recovery is acquiring humility (self-honesty and total self-acceptance) and an attitude of total non-demandingness toward yourself and of the world in general. This recovery-oriented attitude is necessary to overcome a constellation of addiction-promoting irrational attitudes. One of these is what Ellis, McInerney, DiGiuseppe, and Yeager (1988) refer to as "discomfort anxiety." Discomfort anxiety is the inability or unwillingness to tolerate negative feelings, even if it is in one's best interest to do so. This is the trait, for example, that causes smokers to feel like they *need* a cigarette, just because they are feeling some stress or nervousness. A closely related attitude is called "low frustration tolerance." This is referred to in twelve-step meetings as the "King Baby" attitude. Specifically, it is "I want what I want when I want it." Imagine the overeater who cannot resist another doughnut because of this attitude. Note how this attitude, in this example, also overlaps with discomfort anxiety. The third attitude in this constellation is called "short-range hedonism." This is the preference for immediate pleasure in spite of negative long-term consequences. For example, compulsive overeaters know that the next doughnut will work against their goal of weight loss, but they decide, for the moment, that the immediate pleasure is more important.

Perhaps the most important step to recovery from addiction is the recognition of one's loss of control or one's powerlessness to exert control over one's BEHAVIOR OF CHOICE *once the behavior has been initiated.* The difference between people who abuse themselves in some way and people who are addicted to that abuse is that the addicted persons do not or cannot at some point say, "I have had enough." This is due to the powerful influences of what psychologists call "conditioning" as well as neurochemical changes that occur as a result of ingestion of any drug of choice, including alcohol, when chemicals are involved. In some cases of addiction, there may also be a genetic or inherited predisposition to become dependent upon the drug of choice or to the addictive behavior itself.

The term "conditioning" refers to important ways by which we learn. These kinds of learning depend on the principle that we increase the likelihood of doing an action again if that action was last followed by a reward of some kind. A reward is *anything* that makes us FEEL GOOD. This leads to an expectation, whether conscious or unconscious, that doing it again will lead to a similar reward. By the way, it is important to realize that removal of pain or of some other negative condition also serves as a reward in the conditioning process. There is accumulating evidence that genetic predispositions influence how easily one can be conditioned to various kinds of stimuli. Even when chemicals are not involved, the feeling of the high or the removal of the negative feelings brought about by the addictive behavior itself supports the conditioning and *is* the reward.

There are (at least) two major kinds of conditioning. One reinforces our tendency to *feel* a certain way, including emotional reactions and urges to indulge in the addictive/indulgent behaviors. The other reinforces our tendency to *act* in certain ways. This double conditioning is responsible, in great part, for the power of addictions. A permanent chain of conditioned reactions becomes traced in our brains and, like our native language, *never* disappears. It can, however, be substituted (like becoming fluent in a new language) by a more rational chain of conditioned mental-emotional-behavioral reactions, which also can become permanent neural connections. That process of substitution is what this whole program of recovery is about! Recognizing the power and destructiveness of the *chain of addictive conditioned reactions* is essential to overcoming conditioned reactions, and then ultimately to substituting a newly learned chain of conditioned reactions. This means that, at each point in the chain of conditioned reactions, you have a choice. In Chapter 1, we will give an example of a typical chain of conditioned reactions. The lack of recognition of the power of this conditioning or learning process is called "denial."

Almost inadvertently, psychological processes become conditioned at the same time as the behavior. If, for example, you think that what you are doing is wrong, you feel the unease of what psychologists call "cognitive dissonance." This psychological discomfort can be avoided by either *not doing* what you know is wrong, or by *redefining it* as right, at least for the moment. If you can do the former reliably and regularly, then you are not an addict. If you do the latter reliably and predictably, then you are an addict, probably an addict who is in denial. Most active addicts are probably in denial of at least some of the consequences of their acts. Recovery, therefore, primarily depends on breaking through that barrier to sanity.

As we develop an addiction behaviorally, so do we learn the mental attitudinal adjustments that support these behaviors. There is this constant voice in our heads, sometimes soft, sometimes loud, which talks to the parts of our brain that cause our emotional feelings and, eventually, our behavioral reactions to those feelings. When creating an emotion, the voice is stating the kind of attitude, such as evaluations and judgments, we have about what is going on at the moment. The attitude is based upon the beliefs that we hold about ourselves and our world. Thus, we literally talk ourselves through life.

When you were becoming addicted, you were not monitoring that little voice for conscious evaluation, and you learned to deny that what you were doing was wrong or bad for you in the long run. When you had your first cigarette, it probably didn't taste good. You had to learn to like it. Then you heard it is harmful to your health. When some people heard this, they stopped smoking on the spot. Did you? Some people are able to take back control. Almost every addict knows or heard of somebody who just said "No." Of course, for many of them, it was themselves, yesterday. Our guess is that you have probably tried to take control of your habit(s) on your own, one or more times, before reading this book.

In any case, anyone who knows the health risks but continues to smoke uses the psychological mechanism of denial each time he or she lights up. The voice will say "It's alright for me," "I don't smoke enough to worry about it," "One more won't hurt me," "I couldn't live life feeling so deprived," "It hasn't hurt me yet," or most popularly, "Fuck it." These are examples of the irrational ideas that support and maintain any addiction.

You have a clear choice. You can let that little voice rule you forever, or you can take charge of it! This book is about how to take charge of it as well as how to go about making the lifestyle changes necessary to support the new thinking.

Rational-Emotive Behavior Therapy

Again, Rational-Emotive Behavior Therapy, or REBT for short, emphasizes changing thoughts and actions in order to bring feelings and behaviors into a more appropriate adjustment *to reality*. References to the principles of REBT can be found in the reference section at the end of this book. Unlike most forms of psychotherapy, REBT teaches you to become your own therapist. The word *rational* refers to logical and realistic or empirical thinking. It also implies that, for most situations, a probabilistic, rather than an absolutistic (black-and-white) outlook, is most appropriate. **The main characteristic of rational thinking is not to demand that reality conform to your personal wishes and desires.** This includes the reality that there will be uncomfortable feelings, at first, when you choose not to indulge your urges or cravings to continue your addictive behavior. It is unreasonable to expect to be comfortable all of the time. Even nonaddicted people do not feel great all of the time. In the traditional twelve-step program, this non-demandingness is referred to as "humility," which in their program and ours is the antidote to "King Baby" attitudes such as the demand for constant comfort.

A primary ethical principle of REBT is that of *enlightened self-interest*. In brief, this can be summarized as a philosophy of helping others in order to help oneself. The two concepts, *non-demandingness* and *enlightened self-interest*, are, we believe, the underlying bases of both our recovery program and the traditional twelve-step programs, and the key to their success. These principles have been summarized in the Serenity Prayer used both by Albert Ellis, the creator of REBT, and Bill Wilson, the founder of Alcoholics Anonymous:

> God, grant me the serenity to
> accept the things I cannot change,
> the courage to change the things I can,
> and the wisdom to know the difference.

We have altered the prayer slightly. In order to avoid the concept of dependency, we have replaced "God grant me" with "I shall strive for," which emphasizes the concept of taking personal responsibility. We also replaced "courage" with "determination" because it implies

both goal setting and motivation, rather than an absence of
also think of the rational version as a motto, not as a prayer.

﹌ *The Serenity Motto* ﹌

I shall strive for the serenity to
accept the things I cannot change,
the determination to change the things I can,
and the wisdom to know the difference.

The **Twelve Rational-Emotive Behavior Steps to Recovery** are:

1. I admit that I have lost control of my addiction and that my life is becoming unmanageable.

2. I believe that a rational attitude about my life can restore me to sanity.

3. I shall let rational thinking help me.

4. I shall make a searching and fearless inventory of my past decisions and actions.

5. I shall admit to myself and to another human being the exact nature of my wrongs.

6. I am entirely ready to have rational thinking remove all of my shortcomings.

7. I shall apply rational thinking to remove my shortcomings.

8. I shall make a list of all the persons I have harmed, and determine to make amends to them.

9. I shall make amends, wherever possible, except when doing so would injure someone.

10. I shall continue to take my inventory, and when I act wrongly, promptly admit it.

11. I shall seek to improve my conscious contact with reality, striving for the knowledge of what is rational and for the determination to act upon it.

12. Having an increased awareness as a result of what I have accomplished with these steps, I shall practice these principles in all of my affairs, and I will carry this message to others.

In each chapter we include, in addition to our own rational version of the step being discussed, the Alcoholics Anonymous version for the sake of comparison, and our short version of each step for those who prefer an easier way to remember the steps.

Meeting Attendance

While it is possible to work this program without going to a support group, most people will find such groups make their recovery easier. If you choose not to go to a support group, then individual therapy or, even better, group therapy can substitute for a support group. If you choose to use some form of therapy instead of a support group, it would be better if it were an active-directive form of therapy, using cognitive-behavioral principles. Nondirective, client-centered, analytic, or psychodynamic forms of therapy are likely to allow you to avoid confronting your irrational thinking about the addiction. They may also allow you to endlessly avoid reaching your goal of abandoning the addiction.

Support from other people like yourself who are addicted seems to be a helpful part of the recovery process. One of the functions that a group serves is to help keep you honestly looking at yourself and your slippery thinking. If you participate actively in the group, then other group members can confront you when they detect thinking that is supportive of your addiction. A number of organizations exist that provide support and motivation for working your recovery program. This book is written to be used along with virtually all such organized, including but not limited to the following:

Alcoholics Anonymous

Atheists and Agnostics Alcoholics Anonymous

Cocaine Anonymous

Emotions Anonymous

Gamblers Anonymous

Narcotics Anonymous

Nicotine Anonymous

Overeaters Anonymous

Rational Recovery

Secular Organizations for Sobriety

Self Management and Recovery Training

Sex Addicts Anonymous

Sex and Love Addicts Anonymous

Shoppers Anonymous

Workaholics Anonymous

How to Use This Book

While you might benefit, somewhat, from reading straight through this book, we do not recommend approaching your recovery in this manner. In fact, we strongly advise against doing so! It can help you initially to skim the book before you start working the steps, simply to get an idea of what the whole program is about. We do, however, advise you to work through each chapter carefully, doing the exercises as they are recommended. You will note that, in many of the chapters, we advise you to *stop* reading and to do an exercise before proceeding any further. This timing is deliberately arranged so that you can get maximum benefit from the program. If you are in a support group or in psychotherapy, it will greatly aid your recovery to periodically report on your progress in working through this program.

Although there are no deadlines for your recovery, and recovery cannot be rushed, *don't use the book as an excuse to delay recovery.* That is, do not tell yourself that you have to read the entire book and finish all of the exercises before you stop your addictive behaviors. Stop as soon as you can, even if this requires a period of inpatient detoxification, if chemical addiction is what you are working on. Inpatient residence may also be beneficial for nonchemical dependencies in order to take you away from an environment that constantly encourages you to indulge your habit. For chemical and nonchemical dependencies, such a period of time away from your ordinary environment can help you reorient yourself so that you can better resist temptation once you return, or decide that you cannot return, to that environment. If this is not an available option for you, then we strongly recommend daily attendance at support groups, and/or outpatient therapy for the first ninety days of your recovery.

If your addiction is relatively new or relatively mild (you will rate yourself on that in the exercises in Chapter 1), then you might not need the kind of intensive help that we just discussed. In any case, try to stop your addictive behavior as soon as you can, and start working on Chapter 1 today. Do not let anything or anyone discourage you—keep trying and retrying. We wish you much success and happiness.

Chapter One

Understand Loss of Control

Step 1—*I admit that I have lost control of my addiction and that my life is becoming unmanageable.*

The traditional Alcoholics Anonymous statement of Step 1 is:

> We admitted we were powerless over alcohol—
> that our lives had become unmanageable.

Alcoholics Anonymous, and all of the other anonymous groups that sprang up afterwards, say that "we were powerless." In our version of the first step, *powerless* is not used because the word is too often misunderstood to mean that the addicted person cannot do anything about the addiction. Instead, we use the phrase "have lost control." That does not mean to imply that a person cannot do anything to help himself or herself, but simply that one's ability to maintain rational thinking and behavior rapidly diminishes during indulgence in the habit. This is due to the effects of genetic predisposition, conditioning, and neurochemical changes in the brain. Further, the original version of the first step says "our lives have become unmanageable." We use the word *becoming* here, because few persons trying to recover have totally or absolutely lost control over their lives in spite of the fact that it is obvious that they are moving in that direction.

We include in our definition of "addiction" compulsive dependencies on emotional and behavioral habits such as gambling, non-selective promiscuity, self-pity, defensive anger, manipulativeness, risk avoidance, thrill seeking, and so on.

This step challenges the irrational idea that:

> I can do whatever I want without suffering
> any serious negative consequences.

More precisely and completely, Step 1 means that "I admit to myself that I am not behaving in the ways that I think best for me, and I am suffering pain because of this habit and the lifestyle associated with it." That is, it is now both okay and necessary for me to acknowledge that what I thought was either fun or something that I had to or needed to do is NOT the right thing to do because it did not or it does not continue to make me happy, and I cannot predict happiness in the long run if I continue to do it. In fact, I can pretty well predict that if I *do* continue this self-destructive behavior, my life will become a living hell. Thus, what I thought would be forever pleasant or profitable for me in some way is now bringing me unexpected pain or loss of profitability, and I don't like that outcome. Doing it has become more important in my life than makes sense to me, now that I'm honestly thinking about it. It didn't start off being this important! It started out as being fun! How did I let this happen? What shall I do about it?

We sometimes get trained by our own behavior, by influence from friends, family, associates, peers, and from chemicals. Most people are introduced to what later becomes their addiction by people they trust or whose trust or admiration they want. We can be heavily influenced by those around us whom we want to "fit in" with, so we do what we see these people do or believe that they do. Sometimes, we want to impress others, so we try to please them by either doing what they are doing or are interested in, or what we guess they would like from us.

Who doesn't remember the pressures both to conform and to be different while a teenager? We rebelled against both conformity and the ambiguity of being different from others. We didn't really know what to do much of the time. How uncomfortable! As we walk through life, we all find our own basic ways of coping with our feelings of discomfort. Often, the habit we develop is part of our style of coping with feelings. Others of us learned in some way that doing "my thing," whatever it was, made us feel "high" or different from the way we are used to feeling most of the time. Or maybe it made us feel no pain, or feel calm and relaxed, or feel more powerful, or feel much more confident, or feel a delicious "rush." And we started to go for this feeling, or for combinations of such feelings, thereby altering the direction of at least parts of our lives to attain it.

Step 1 is a hard one! To admit to having given the control of some of your own actions over to a habit can be a startling event. Does it make you think that you are a failure if this is true? Or "no good"? This is not a time to take a moralistic look at yourself or your habit; but it is a time for strict honesty, without which you have no chance at recovery. Sure, you can deny that the habit is "that bad" for a while. *Take the time to do Exercises 1-1 and 1-2 now.* They are at the end of the chapter. Be as self-searching and as honest as you can. Your life or your sanity may depend on it.

What do the exercises tell you? Is pursuing the habitual behavior positive enough (the sum from Exercise 1-2) to trade off for what is on your list of negative results (the sum from Exercise 1-1)? If your answer is "Yes," then give this book to a deserving friend so you can indulge yourself until you get the feeling that you are at "rock bottom." You are unlikely to succeed in beating your habit if you are not doing it for yourself, no matter who else may benefit from your changes. If you are trying to change in order to keep your job or to keep your spouse in your life, you may have a clash of values set up within yourself. You must determine for yourself whether the importance of the negative effects of the habit (Exercise 1-1) is greater than the importance of its positive aspects (Exercise 1-2). If so, then you can change your life by following this program. As you continue to make additions to these lists of consequences, it is likely that indulgence will seem increasingly less worthwhile, and your motivation to follow this program will increase.

The word *unmanageable* in Step 1 means that there are things going on that you did not plan to happen to you. You may decide, for example, to take your paycheck directly to the bank so you can pay your bills, but instead you make yourself feel compelled to go to a racetrack or a drug dealer. Then, you spend your whole check at the place you swore to yourself that you wouldn't visit. That is unmanageability! Or you say to yourself, "I'll just buy a ten-dollar bag of dope and go home," but you start to use it on the spot and proceed to buy twenty more bags and run out of money before you are done. That is unmanageability. Or you say, "I can't help it but I just have to have one of these delicious-looking pieces of cake." Then you finish the cake. That is unmanageability.

It is probably true that in the past you made such decisions and carried them out easily and without much thought. That was BEFORE you became addicted to your behavior of choice. Now that you have trained yourself that payday means time to gamble, seduce somebody, go to the liquor store or drug dealer, and that it is followed by that "special feeling" you get upon culminating your habit, things are different for you forever. So, too, for habits such as smoking and overeating. You are now caught up in a long chain of repetitive conditioned behaviors supported by reward and, possibly, your individual genetic predisposition. To break the spell, you need to make certain changes in your lifestyle and in your beliefs, especially those that are about what is good for you.

The result of comparing the number from Exercise 1-1 with that of Exercise 1-2 gives you an idea of how difficult it may be to do the work that will help you beat your habit. The greater the number from Exercise 1-1 is, as compared to the number from Exercise 1-2, the easier it will be. But if this difficulty score is high, do not let it discourage you. You can still be successful if you are determined enough and are willing to think rationally and to accept the help of others. Remember that there is a constellation of three addiction-promoting traits that will try to defeat you at this point. They are discomfort anxiety, low frustration tolerance, and short-range hedonism. Refer to the Introduction and Glossary for definitions of these terms if you need to. Throughout this book, we will show you how to change these traits or attitudes.

The Chain of Addictive Conditioned Reactions

As we mentioned in the Introduction, every addiction sets up—or in essence, actually is—a chain of conditioned reactions in your brain. Each link in the chain represents new connections among hundreds or thousands of brain cells. Once these neurological links are made, they cannot be unmade! All of the connections occur as a result of the good, rewarding, feeling (high) that you get from the substance or the activity to which you are addicted.

There are two kinds of conditioning (or learning) that create these connections. One of them causes a permanent change in the way you feel about things related to your addiction. The other causes permanent changes in the way you behave or act toward things related to your addiction. The process of conditioning causes the high to be anticipated or preceded by a change in feelings which, in turn, changes behavior. Alcoholics, for example, feel and act very differently than nonalcoholics when they see a bottle of their favorite beverage. Shopping addicts feel and act differently from nonaddicted people when they receive a catalog in the mail, window shop, or tune into one of the multitude of TV shopping channels. Initially, only the drink itself or the purchased item causes the high, which may be a feeling of relaxation or a feeling of excitement. Eventually, however, many associations begin to bring on some of the same feelings, which later get labeled as urges to follow through with related acts. You see a piece of chocolate and you can almost taste it, which can easily lead you to want it right away. You order a drink at a bar and immediately become relaxed. You see something heavily discounted at the mall, become excited, and you buy it even though you don't need it. As the chain of related associations forms, it *becomes* the addiction. This group or chain of associated reactions affects large and important areas of the addict's life. Our analysis of the typical chain of conditioning follows. Please note that the chain of conditioned addictive reactions comes from our analysis of thousands of addicts' direct reports of their thoughts, feelings, and behaviors.

The first link in the chain is what psychologists call a "stimulus." Addicts are taught to call it a "trigger." Once the chain is fully developed, this trigger can be the thought of or the sight of the desired substance or object; a location associated with the substance, object, or behavior; being with people who encourage the addictive behavior; by having some "extra" money; or even the time of day or the day of the week.

The second link in the chain is what psychologists call "irrational thinking," and what twelve-stepping addicts are taught to call "stinking thinking." Examples are: "One more won't hurt me." "I deserve it." "If I'm a little late with the rent it'll be okay, so I can afford it today." "I need it." "I can't help myself." "I have to have it."

Then the stinking thinking leads to the third link in the chain, which is a combination of the urge and the decision to indulge in the habit. Note that, in the nonaddicted person, the first link does not necessarily lead to the second link. In the addicted person, the second link occurs automatically, and is already beginning to get the addict "high." That is, the addict is enjoying the stinking thinking that he or she knows will lead to a decision to indulge the habit. This enjoyment of the irrational thinking *is* the urge to indulge the habit.

The fourth link is the first actual action or *behavior* in the chain of addictive conditioned reactions. That is, it is the first thing that you *do*, other than think or feel. We call it "the arrangement" or, if the decision to use is unconscious, "the setup." The setup will be explained later. The arrangement is the conscious planning that ultimately leads to the addict's desired result. This can be a call to a dealer. It can be a call to a friend to go shopping or drinking. It can be cashing a check. It can be getting a baby-sitter. It can be looking in the paper to see when the first race starts. Or it can be a call to your spouse explaining why you'll be late tonight (usually a lie).

As the arrangement progresses, there is a continuous interaction among thinking, feeling, and behavior. The urge increases and the behavior moves inexorably toward the ultimate goal: indulgence in the habit and the high that it produces. From this point on, the addict is progressively losing control. If the progression is not inter-rupted during the stinking-thinking stage, it becomes more and more difficult to stop as the chain continues link by link.

The sequence of events, from this point on, can differ from one addiction to another. We call the fifth link "locating." It's simply the act of going to the place at which the habit will be indulged or the product purchased. This could be the dealer, the bar, the store, the race track or casino, the house of prostitution, or to a TV set or refrigerator.

The sixth link is "the purchase," although for some the purchase might already have been made earlier. Whether the purchase is done at this point or at an earlier point, it is instructive to recognize that even the act of handing out your hard-earned money to do something that eventually hurts you might have made you feel good for a while. Many recovering drug and alcohol addicts have told us that the "extra" money they have left over as a result of not purchasing (spending as a result of or in preparation for indulgence in the addictive habit) "burns a hole in my pocket." They get so excited when they have cash on hand that they easily become shopping or gambling addicts. They have learned to enjoy, or get high from the very act of spending money. In recovery lingo, this is often referred to as *cross addiction* and is something to be taken seriously, especially by people in early recovery.

The seventh link is "receiving." This, of course, applies to drug abuse, alcoholism, shopping, smoking, and overeating, but not necessarily to other habits such as gambling unless the gambler is playing the lotto or betting on horses, on or off track, or gambling with casino chips. Usually, by this time, the addict is feeling pretty good. He or she has that "needed" pack of cigarettes, the bag of chocolate cookies, or the bag of cocaine, methamphetamine, or heroin, and is feeling happily excited or relaxed.

The eighth link is "preparation." Again, this link may or may not apply to your particular habit. The heroin addict, for example, may have to "cook" the heroin before using it. The cocaine addict used to have to go through an elaborate ritual in order to free-base it, but the availability of crack has made getting ready to get high much simpler. Hail to technology! The overeater, of course, might prepare a gourmet meal or simply rip open a bag of munchies. The racing addict (gambler) has to make his or her betting selections, but this has usually been done before the sixth link.

The ninth link is what all of the process has really been about— "indulging." This includes using the drug of choice, gorging, placing a bet and watching the race or the football game, waiting for "the number" to come up, or having sex.

The tenth link, of course, is the high itself. That is the *feeling* that has forged the entire chain of conditioned reactions. The high is always a pleasurable feeling, but it differs greatly from one habit to another. It can be a feeling of excitement or stimulation, a feeling of joy or ecstasy, a feeling of relaxation or tension reduction, a feeling of being at peace with the whole world, a feeling of being superior or godlike, or it can be an orgasm.

The eleventh link is "substance-affected behavior," which can be markedly different from one's normal behavior. Frequently, it brings one back all the way to the sixth link, which is spending still more money on the indulgence. Often, as is usually the case with alcohol and many drugs, it is simply stupid behavior that feels good to the addict at the time, but usually irritates others. In retrospect, this is frequently the reason why people would like to stop their addiction. Somehow, however, no matter how insane the substance-affected behavior is, it almost never seems to be, in itself, enough for the addict to cease and desist. This is because once behavior is rewarded (feeling good is a potent reward), it is most often not affected by later punishment. We can see this easily in children when they persist in jumping up and down on the bed, even though they are later yelled at or spanked for that behavior. A person is only motivated to stop acting a certain way if punishment is the immediate consequence of the act. That's the principle that makes Antabuse, a drug that interacts with alcohol to make you feel sick, effective for some alcoholics. If alcoholics regularly take their Antabuse and begin to feel sick instead of feeling delightfully relaxed or pleasantly drunk when having a drink, the chain of conditioned reactions is thus interfered with.

The twelfth link is "the letdown." The punitive effects of the substance-affected behavior, while they do not stop the behavior, usually result in a variety of bad feelings once the conditioned chain of reactions has run its course. Often, this is when the addict seeks help or treatment. However, equally often, he or she decides to get high again in order to alleviate feelings of guilt, shame, worthlessness, hopelessness, and depression.

Because of the associated pleasure, each link reinforces the one before it. The high strengthens the tendency to use the drug (this is the first kind of conditioning) and causes the acts leading to the high to feel good in themselves (this is the second kind of conditioning). Thus, the alcoholic starts to feel relaxed on the first sip, even before the alcohol has entered the bloodstream or reached the pleasure centers in the brain. Then, using the alcohol reinforces the act of preparation that preceded it, such as mixing or pouring the drink. That act in itself, now is a source of pleasure. And, link by link, the chain of conditioned reactions, which is the neurological representation of the addiction, is formed in the addict's brain. Every time the habit is indulged, the chain therefore gets stronger until the neurological links are fully formed.

We hope that the chain of addictive conditioned reactions illustrates for you what leads to the traditional twelve-step concept of "powerless," our concept of "lost control." The two kinds of conditioning, and the ineffectiveness of the influence of later negative results in many areas of life that are affected by the addiction, all contribute to loss of control. In order to regain control, you will need to build a more healthful chain of conditioned reactions as an alternative. Exercises 1-3 and 1-4 in this chapter will help you begin this process, but don't complete them until we instruct you to do so.

Think of powerlessness and loss of control, for either version of Step 1, this way. It means that relative to the influence of our habit, our willpower amounts to naught. Obviously, any addictive or compulsive habit or substance can be substituted for the word *alcohol* in the steps. Telling yourself that you "shouldn't do it" is of little or no value for controlling the behavior.

Picture this! You are on the top floor of a tall building. Someone you respect or admire asks you, politely, to jump out of the window. Would you do it? Of course not! Did it take lots and lots of thought to make this decision? Why not? You know that if you comply with that request you will squash yourself on the pavement below and will be dead forever! That's why not!! Once you have jumped, you are powerless to slow your fall and the results will be unmanageable. Therefore, no willpower is needed to resist the act even if you would really *love* to be able to fly! A deep conviction that you have lost control can help you develop the same kind of immediate, reflexive response toward your habitual behavior of choice—whether it be about heroin, picking your nose in public, placing a two-dollar bet on a horse, or whatever—that you have toward jumping out of that window. The best response, as an alternative to indulging your habit, will ultimately become your positive goal.

Here are some examples of positive responses to temptations or "triggers":

Smoking	"I want to breathe better" "I want to taste my food better"
Drugs/Alcohol	"I want to be sober today" "I want to live and be healthy"
Overeating	"I want to look nicer" "I want to be healthier"
Gambling	"I want the money in my pocket" "I want to earn my way rather than rely on luck or chance"
Sex	"I want someone who loves me" "I want to feel good and have fun rather than feel hurt or used"

Obviously, this list could be endless! The point is that it is good eventually to get to the point of responding in the way you want to, no matter what the habit. Substitute your own goal(s) and practice rehearsing your reflexive statement. This is your major gain from changing your habit. Visualize yourself as having already attained the goal, and savor how good it feels. It takes lots and lots of rehearsal to get it together and even more to make it reflexive. Until the reflex reaction is automatic, carry a copy of your list from Exercise 1-1, the list of what you want to avoid by changing your habit.

The only problem with the concept of "powerlessness" is that too many people interpret it to mean that they are powerless to change their habits and/or their lives and therefore cannot live without the habit. Thus, the rational interpretation of Step 1 says, "I have lost control of my addiction." You are, in fact, far from powerless over your own acts. Once you begin indulging yourself in the habit, THEN you lose or give up control. Only you can prevent yourself from coming to the point of such powerlessness. If you follow these steps you will win, and the habitual behavior will lose in the long run.

You are never powerless to resist beginning to indulge in your habit, even though resistance can be difficult. But, once you begin to indulge, the urge to continue, if you are addicted, becomes stronger. In addition, the excitement over reaching the high becomes stronger and impairs your ability to think rationally. Finally, if your habit is substance abuse, there is a direct neurochemical effect that further reduces your capacity to think rationally and, therefore, to control your behavior.

Due to different histories of conditioning, modeling after others, and personality characteristics—some of which have a strong genetic component—some people are more susceptible to these effects than others. For these people the effort required to control their indulgence is not worth it. It is far easier for them to abstain altogether. If you can set a limit for yourself that provides pleasure with few or no negative consequences and stick to that limit on a consistent basis, then you are not addicted—you are not powerless. After two or three drinks, the social drinker can say, "I've had enough; if I drink more I'll feel sick or act stupidly, so I'd better stop"—and *mean* it. The alcoholic wants just a taste at first, wants a buzz next, then wants to *really* get high, and finally opts for oblivion. His or her limit occurs only *after* severe negative consequences, like passing out or getting punched out by another drunk at the bar. For the social, or normal, drinker the limit occurs *before* the negative consequences occur. Thus, it is not so much the degree of indulgence that defines addiction, as whether or not the tendency to indulge tends to increase once the habit is initiated. Loss of control (or "powerlessness" properly used) refers to an increasing tendency to engage in the habit after it has begun. If that is your pattern, stop fooling yourself and realize that *not starting* is the easiest way not to go too far. Whenever you want to indulge, remember (1) that you will most likely indulge too much ("one is too many, a thousand is not enough"), and (2) the ultimate results are too painful to be worth the indulgence.

To reiterate, loss of control and powerlessness means that once you start engaging in your habit of choice, you do not have the capacity or the ability to set reasonable (to you) limits on that consumptive behavior. What this means ultimately, if you are ever going to recover from your burden in life, is that YOU HAD BEST NOT EVER BEGIN to indulge yourself in whatever the habit may be. NOT EVEN JUST A LITTLE BIT. NOT JUST THIS ONE TIME. Once you have acquired the condition of addiction, *you have lost that privilege* of dibbing, dabbing, chipping, or indulging in the habit. If you are going to remain a recovering addict (as opposed to an active or practicing addict), you HAD BEST NEVER AGAIN do the act that hurts you. This is true whether the act be popping heroin, overeating, or playing the lottery! This is true NO MATTER HOW YOU FEEL at the moment. Moments of urging or craving will pass, even if you do nothing at all about it (which is not what we recommend!).

There are two kinds of addictions that do not require total abstinence: overeating and sex. With overeating, obviously, eating must continue, but once you have chosen an appropriate diet, preferably with the help of your primary health care provider or a specialist, stick strictly to it. You might need a well-defined period of time to ease into the diet, but then do not deviate from it. Only in this way can you regain control over your eating behavior. For sexual addiction, we strongly recommend a period of total abstinence, for at least a month or until your support or therapy group, individual therapist, or sponsor believe you are ready to resume well-defined, specific, and thus limited sexual activity. Then determine which sexual activities are appropriate for you, and do not deviate from them. If you are working this program with no outside support, you will, of course, have to make this decision on your own. Please err on the side of being conservative! In our many years of helping addicts recover, we have noted that numerous drug addicts and alcoholics are also sex addicts. Frequently, they started their drug or alcohol habit in order to make gaining sexual access easier for them. Thus, for many addicts of different kinds, an initial period of sexual abstinence is a good idea, at least until they have a good grasp of, and have made progress on, their recovery program for substance addiction.

There are some habits for which "cold turkey" is a dangerous path to quitting, and thus a regimen of tapering off, with or without medical help, is called for before you can consider yourself "in recovery." This is especially the case for alcohol, opiates, some tranquilizers and sleeping medications, and some pain relievers.

The Alcoholics Anonymous Big Book says that you should be willing to *go to any length* to beat your addiction. This is completely rational and logical! This means that you must do whatever it is that you *personally require* to avoid the traps of your addiction. This usually means that your life will be far easier if you avoid certain people, places, and things. This is a motto that will carry you very far into recovery. But there is a lot more to it than this!

The Big Book says that addiction is "cunning, baffling, powerful." This is a statement about the way in which denial works. *Denial* enables us to talk ourselves into doing precisely what we know we shouldn't be doing. This process is not always conscious, but the chain of addictive conditioned reactions continues to unfold anyhow. The following illustrates what we call the *setup*. Imagine, for example, a newly recovering alcoholic, sitting with his wife, restlessly switching from one TV channel to another. He is beginning to want a drink, but he doesn't know that. His wife says to him, "Honey, are you okay? You seem nervous."

He snaps back, "I'm fine!"

She says, "Okay. I was just concerned that maybe you were feeling like having a drink."

He says, angrily, "Look. Don't try to run my program!"

She says, feeling hurt, "I was just trying to help. Don't get angry at me. It's your problem!"

He says, "I gotta get out of here and cool off before we have a blowout!" He slams the door on his way out and gets into his car. He's thinking, "If anyone can drive me back to drinking, it sure is her." He starts driving, with no intended destination, getting angrier and angrier at her, until the car stops, as if by magic, at his favorite bar. The rest of the story, you already know. He thinks, when he enters the bar, that he is just at that moment deciding to have a drink. But actually, his decision to relapse was made while he was fiddling with the remote control. Then he set up the scene to give himself an excuse to drink one more time. This is why the disease is called "cunning, baffling, and powerful."

There are many ways in which you, the addict, thinking that you are working against the addiction, are actually moving in the direction of relapse. One such way is for you to demand abstinence or sobriety of yourself by saying, "I know I shouldn't drink anymore." Of course, "shouldn't-ing" is a major part of the problem. If you would consider what is *good* or *better* for you in the long run instead of thinking about what you *should* or *should not* do, you would do far fewer self-destructive acts. Demandingness, in other words, often results in the opposite of its intended result. When you *demand that you stop* your habit, telling yourself, "I shouldn't do this any more," but *don't actually stop*, you have lost control!

Consider this. As we grew up, we were always being told by our parents, teachers, and clergy what it is that we should and should not be doing, or even want to do, some of the time. Of course, this had little to do with what we *felt* like doing. Thus, we learned to be vigilant for who was, or who might be, watching; and when we thought that no one important to us was there watching, we did what *we* wanted to do, hoping all the while not to get caught. There was even a thrill of some sort, even if it was just relief, when we got away with doing what we knew or suspected that we shouldn't have done, according to the rules. Many addicts of all kinds have made this kind of thinking into a game as they approached, or while going through, adulthood. Thus, advancing chronological age does not mean that we no longer act like children. When we indulge ourselves in our habit of choice, we are doing something childish. Meanwhile, no matter how strongly we believe that we SHOULD or SHOULDN'T do something, we still have this mechanism, learned in childhood, of trying to get away with doing it anyway or doing it OUR way, believing ourselves to be exempt from the usually serious consequences for doing whatever it may be, *this* time.

Thus, when we believe that we SHOULDN'T or MUSTN'T do something, the infantile rebellion comes into play as a conditioned response from our own history. This makes us think, usually unconsciously, "I'll show you! I'll do it, but THIS TIME I'll still be okay." The Anonymous groups call this stinking thinking. We call it nonsensical, childish, and irrational.

By this time, we hope that you can agree with the short version of Step 1, which is:

I can't handle this bullshit anymore!

Here, bullshit refers to whatever addictive behavior you engage in as well as any addictive substance, including too much of the wrong foods for you, with which you indulge yourself.

Now, please complete Exercises 1-3 and 1-4.

Now that you have completed these two exercises, you will have discovered whether or not you have lost control over your habit. If you found that you have lost control over your habit, you have probably also found that its negative consequences strongly outweigh its positive consequences. If that is the case, you are ready to proceed to the rest of this chapter.

In order to make sure that you are not deluding yourself about whether you have multiple addictive behaviors, it would be best to compare your behavior in one area with that in others. That is, you might be accepting the fact that your drinking is out of control but fooling yourself about your gambling. The fifth exercise for Chapter 1 allows you to match all of your habits with each other on a scale of 0 (no problem) to 10 (you have hit bottom). You will want to complete Exercises 1-1 through 1-4 on every habit you score 3 or more on in Exercise 1-5. You don't necessarily have to do that or work on all twelve steps on all of your addictions at once! Do the whole program on one or more of those addictions according to your personal level of readiness at this time. As you make progress on one problem, you might find yourself deciding that it is time to start working on some of the others.

It's your life. It's up to you. So go at your own pace, handling whatever you feel ready to handle. Maybe you will start work on drinking and overeating this year, smoking and gambling next year, and workaholism two or three years from now.

To be fair, however, we had best warn you that *all* chemical dependencies (drugs and alcohol) are best worked on all at once because of the phenomenon of "cross-addiction" or substitution. This can occur with any two addictions, but is more common among the addictions to chemicals. It is common, for example, for a controlled drinker who gets hooked on cocaine to become alcoholic after giving up cocaine. Whichever path you choose, if you find one "bad habit" increasing as you give up another, you had best start working on that one, too! For more specific advice concerning multiple addictions, see Chapter 14. If you are confused about where to start, read that chapter now. Now, complete Exercise 1-5 and, taking the first step toward a better life, give up *at least one* of your self-defeating, irrational, neurotic dependencies. It takes time and effort, but *you can do it!*

Chapter 1 Exercises

At this point, the forces that brought you to this place in your life are irrelevant! What you need to do now is decide whether or not you are ready to do whatever it will take for you to change your self-destructive behaviors. If so, then proceed, and get ready to buckle down and work on setting goals and mustering the determination to reach them. These are designed to help you make this important decision. They are *not* optional. They are the most important part of the program.

We strongly recommend that you purchase a spiral-bound, ruled notebook to have a single place to keep the written exercises you will be doing as a part of this recovery program. The exercises in some chapters require that you refer back to previously done exercises, and some exercises cannot be completed all at one time. Thus, having them conveniently in one place will make working your recovery program a little bit easier. In the future, it may also serve as a memento of all of the hard work that you have put into your recovery efforts. Further, it can serve as a valuable reference to fall back upon at times when you are feeling tempted to relapse.

ᲔᲗ   *Exercise 1-1*   ᲔᲗ

Write a list of the negative consequences you have had so far (the things that caused you either physical or psychological pain), and of those things that are likely to cause you such pains in the future, as a result of indulging in your habit. Leave this list someplace convenient, because it is not usually possible to do it in one sitting. This assignment is something to think—and keep thinking—about. You may also add to it over time, as more negative things actually happen to you, and as you keep considering the probable future consequences of your habit. It is possible that the *potential* negative consequences of your habit may be even more important than those that you have already experienced as a result of your habit. *These are your ONLY reasons for working on changing those attitudes and behaviors that have been so important in your life.*

Next, rate each consequence in your list as to HOW MUCH PAIN it caused or still causes for you. Use a scale of 0 to 100, where 100 is the most painful thing that you can imagine, and 0 is no pain at all. Note that if little or no emotional pain is associated with the consequence, then it is not really a negative consequence and would best be scratched off the list. When you have rated all of your consequences, sum the ratings.

✌ *Exercise 1-2* ✌

Write a list of the positive, life-enhancing features of your habit. Later, you will be asked to think of alternative ways to satisfy some of these gratifying experiences. These are your reasons for continuing the habit *and* your reasons for relapsing. Some of these things you may sorely miss. Leave this list around as instructed in Exercise 1-1. Keep thinking about what you will miss.

Next, rate each feature as to how much pleasure it adds to your life. Use a scale of 0 to 100 as in Exercise 1-1. Add the pleasure scores together. This score will tell you how much emotional pain or discomfort to expect in the early part of your recovery as a result of giving up these pleasurable effects of your addiction.

ᴧ *Exercise 1-3* ᴧ

What is it that triggers the feeling that it is time to indulge in the habit? To do this exercise effectively, carry a small notebook or journal, and note when you feel urges or cravings to indulge in the habit. This can also be done in your regular notebook if you typically carry it with you. Note the day, date, place, time, and what it is that you think happened to bring on that feeling. More specifically, what were you thinking at the time that the urge hit you? You will learn from this both the temporal patterns of your addiction, if there are any, and the environmental stimuli or circumstances that you are conditioned to respond to by having the urge or craving. This is the first link in the chain of addictive conditioned reactions. You will also get a handle on your stinking thinking, the second link in the chain.

Write a list of changes that you ALREADY know you will have to make in order to break the habit. Think about the people, places, and things that turn your habit on. Are you willing to make such changes? Rate each thing on a scale of 0 to 100, with 0 being anything you stubbornly refuse to change because you think it will wreck your life, and 100 being something so obviously important to change that you will be determined to stop before finishing reading this sentence. Remember that it is these changes that will create a new chain of conditioned reactions in your brain as a substitute for the addiction chain.

Also keep this list around. You will be adding to it as you work the steps!

ༀ *Exercise 1-4* ༀ

Categories of addictive behavior:

1.	alcohol	11.	shopping
2.	tobacco	12.	stealing
3.	exercise	13.	sleep
4.	sweets	14.	television
5.	gambling	15.	telephone
6.	sex	16.	prescription drugs
7.	work	17.	binges
8.	a sport	18.	illegal drugs
9.	romance	19.	using the Internet
10.	reading	20.	other _____

For each *one* of the nineteen potentially addictive behaviors listed here (feel free to add more as needed), list your answers to each of the ten questions (symptoms or criteria of irrational dependence) that follow, as they apply to you. Give each "yes" answer a score of 1, and each "no" answer a 0. For each category, add your scores for the ten questions. You will then have a total score from 0 (no problem) to 10 (serious addictive problem) for each addictive behavior. Please note that any human behavior, even if it is usually a normal or healthful activity, can be considered an addiction if it earns a score of 3 or more. Perhaps you'll score 7 for cocaine, 8 for smoking, and 9 for sex. Because it is *your choice* whether or not to give up any of these addictions, that is, those on which your score is 3 or more, it makes no sense to be dishonest. *You* have the choice as to whether you want to give up cocaine while increasing your tobacco consumption and being more promiscuous! Only you can make that choice; so be honest with yourself first, so that you can make informed choices with the facts at hand instead of in the fog of minimization and denial.

The questions: answer yes or no for each of the categories above:

1. Do you continue the use or the behavior in spite of social, occupational, psychological, or physical problems?

2. Do you continue the use or the behavior in physically dangerous situations?

3. Do you lose control, i.e., do you indulge in larger amounts or for longer periods of time than intended?

4. Do you need at least 50 percent more of the substance or behavior in order to get the same effect that you used to, OR do you get less effect from the same amount?

5. Are you unable to cut down or control the indulgent behavior?

6. Do you spend much time obtaining substances or tools for the indulgent behavior, OR recovering from the effects of the behavior?

7. Are you frequently high or withdrawing, physically or psychologically (for example, thinking about it) during important activities at work, school, or home.

8. Have you given up important social, work, interpersonal, or recreational activities due to the indulgent behavior?

9. Do you experience withdrawal symptoms (depression, agitation, insomnia, fatigue, poor concentration) after extensive indulgence?

10. Do you often use the indulgent behavior to avoid or relieve withdrawal symptoms?

Scoring:

ABUSE   1 or 2 "Yes" answers
MILD Addiction   3 or 4 "Yes" answers
MODERATE Addiction   5 to 8 "Yes" answers
SEVERE Addiction   9 or 10 "Yes" answers

∽ *Exercise 1-5* ∽

Give up one addictive habit. If you are not ready to give one up completely, at least reduce your indulgence in one habit. There will be no significant learning if you don't change your behavior. As Benjamin Franklin once said, "If there are no pains, there are no gains." Reduce or eliminate whichever habit you can at this point. If you are unable to reduce or give up even one of your habits now, proceed to Chapter 2 to learn more about how to do so.

In order to facilitate reducing one of your habits, we recommend charting your indulgence on a day-to-day basis. What this involves, for example, is writing the dates of the month, line by line, on a page in your notebook. Then, for each date, make a tote mark for each time you indulge in your habit that day. At the end of each row (day), write the total number of times that you indulged or overindulged. For some addictions, the obvious daily goal is zero or an easily set number of tote marks. For counting cigarettes, the number of times you snorted or shot up, consuming cookies, or drinking bottles of beer, this is an easy and unambiguous task of simple counting. For other habits, however, you may have to adjust your way of counting the number of transgressions into your habit. We assume that you will *know* when you have overeaten, made inappropriate passes at others, bought things you really didn't need, and so forth. These are the things to record in your behavior chart. For overeating, you may set a goal of some number of calories or fat or carbohydrate grams per day. Then you must decide how many calories, or fat or carbohydrate grams, above your allowed amounts equals one tote mark.

For sex, you might use a tote mark for each act that you consider to be inappropriate or in excess of what you think is reasonable for you. In some cases of sexual addiction, the issue is not the number of acts, but rather the time spent in sexual behavior. Thus, you might have determined that it is normal or healthful for you to spend fifteen minutes masturbating per day. In that case, every additional fifteen minutes would warrant a tote mark.

For gambling, the issue is probably not how many bets you place each day, but rather how much money you bet each day. You have to determine how many dollars warrants a tote mark. If you bet on horses, two dollars is probably a reasonable amount to warrant a tote mark; if you play the slots, then the number of quarters over your goal amount would warrant a mark; if you play the lottery, then one dollar could warrant a tote mark. Using the dollar method of toting eliminates the possibility that you can tell yourself, "I only bet once today, so that's not too bad," when in fact, it was a thousand-dollar bet on a single race or hand of cards.

The purpose of this daily record is, of course, to keep you honest with yourself about how much progress you are making. You can set your own pace, but what you want to be able to see is a relatively continuous decrease in the indulgence in your habit, down to zero. Remember that you only record a tote mark when you exceed your self-set goal for the day.

Chapter Two

Take Reality as Authority

Step 2—*I believe that a rational attitude about my life can restore me to sanity.*

The traditional Alcoholics Anonymous version of this step is:

> Came to believe that a Power greater than
> ourselves could restore us to sanity.

In our version of Step 2, rationally interpreting reality is substituted for reliance on a higher power such as God. *Reality* is where we live, whether we like it or not. Reality is the *objective understanding* of the here and now, as well as of the past. The future is but a fantasy. What is objective understanding? It is the appreciation of the reality that everything that has happened *has happened*, and that these facts may have nothing to do with what we wish would have happened, or what we think or believe should have happened. This idea reaches into the future as well. Rationally, whatever will happen is exactly what *should* happen, even if we don't like whatever it may be. Having a rational attitude is, therefore, accepting reality as it is. Adopting such an attitude will help you overcome the fantasy world of your addiction. You *can* learn to think more rationally.

This step challenges the irrational idea that:

> There is nothing that I can do to help myself
> be a more sane, more happy, person.

This idea is based on the illogical premise that "I must, have to, need to, or should continue to think, feel, and act the way I usually have in the past." One of the most difficult clients we have ever worked with, Roseanne, a sex addict and group therapy member, was fond of saying, "People never really change." She often gave examples of how people she knew vowed to diet, stop smoking, become less verbally abusive, and so forth. Although we recognized that she was presenting familiar examples of the great difficulty in changing oneself, we have many times, over the thirty-plus years of our clinical and personal experience, seen people who have, in fact, made profound changes in their lives. These people all had to accept Steps 1 and 2 before being able to do so. That is, they first had to accept that their current psychological condition was unacceptable to them and was poisoning their lives. Second, they had to accept that they could help themselves by changing their attitudes as well as their behaviors. They were then in a position to be able to start challenging the self-defeating *shoulds* that lead to most of their problems. Interestingly, Roseanne worked hard at changing herself, and she eventually adopted a much healthier attitude toward life, felt better about herself, and abandoned her nonselective promiscuity.

Recall, from the Introduction, that one of the main characteristics of rational thinking is that it is nondemanding. Demandingness is a style of thinking that is usually expressed by words such as *should, need, must, got to, have to,* and *ought.* These expressions of demandingness carry with them inordinate and unjustifiable amounts of personal value or importance. They imply an absolute insistence, rather than a mere expression of opinions or preferences that reality be different from the way it is. It is rational for me to have the opinion that I prefer it not to rain on a day that I want to have a picnic. This opinion or preference has a relative, rather than an absolute, value for me. It is not a belief that it is absolutely mandatory that it not rain. It might be a mild preference for sunshine or a strong preference. If, on the other hand, I were to demand that it not rain, that would represent 100 percent of the possible emotional value or importance that I could muster up. Thus, if it does rain, then the resultant feeling would be the very worst, strongest feeling that I could possibly have.

The absolutistic demand, in violation of reality as it is, would therefore cause me great distress, possibly leading me to feel inconsolably depressed or uncontrollably enraged. Obviously, no picnic is worth such torture, but this is the kind of reaction to which demandingness often leads us. This is because demandingness almost always represents a 100 percent conviction that our way is the only way reality has a right to be. Addicts have told us, for example, "If I can't have another cigarette, I'll go crazy." "If I couldn't have my heroin, life wouldn't be worthwhile." "I'd rather die than not be able to place another bet." In each of these cases, the underlying irrational thinking was that they must, need, or have to have or do something that they enjoy. Thus, their recreational activity has become an addiction. Thinking in terms of preferences supports healthful, enjoyable activities. Thinking in terms of demands supports addictions.

Among the terms used to express demandingness, "should" is probably at the top of the list. A way to work around misusing this popular word is to define it in a special way. The concept of "SHOULD" had best be reserved to refer to TRUTH and REALITY. For example, the weather tomorrow should be whatever it is going to be, no matter how I would like it to be. This means that every-thing that has ever happened is what *should* have been, and that everything that will happen will happen as it should. This does not imply that you, I, or any other human being will *like* what happens. The opposite of "shoulding" is "accepting."

ACCEPTING your life **as it really is** is necessary for you to be optimally happy. Again, this does *not* mean *liking* this reality. Lack of acceptance means **insisting and demanding** that your reality be dif-ferent from what it actually is. *Acceptance* means examining the sit-uation and deciding whether or not you like it the way it is. Our best advice is continually to attempt to alter or change reality to meet or approximate your own personal standards—that is, to make your reality more like you want it to be—but don't *demand* that the changes occur.

The changes you would like are often not possible. Even when they are, sometimes it takes a long time to make things the way you would most like them to be, or it is too expensive, either in terms of your finances or your effort. You had best be motivated by your dis-like of a situation rather than by your lack of acceptance of the same situation. Otherwise, you are likely to remain disturbed in some way (upset, angry, depressed, anxious, etc.) because you are not accept-ing what you do not like.

Reality is absolute! Neither your opinion nor mine influences what reality is. If a tree falls in the forest, it falls whether we like it or not, and whether anyone hears it or not.

When we learn that a behavior of ours is out of control, that is *the reality*, but neither we nor the people around us need to like this fact of reality. In fact, often we think it is too hard to change the out-of-control behavior, and we convince ourselves that we are defeated before we even begin to try to change the behavior.

What is needed here is a long-range view of ourselves both with the behavior in our lives and without the behavior in our lives. Looking at both of them, the question to ask is: "What is better for me in the long run?" Recognizing that you would be better off by changing the out-of-control behavior and considering how deeply better your life could be has the power to develop a *desire* or *wish* to alter the behavior. This is what you can capitalize upon!

You have probably, when not into total denial of the behavior as a problem, thought to yourself that you SHOULD stop. Most people with addictive behaviors have done this. However, since most of us were raised by being told by authority figures (parents, teachers, clergy, etc.) what we **should** and **shouldn't** be doing, we learned long ago to set these authoritarian demands aside so that we could go and do what we wanted to do. Always, what you *want* to do will have more long-lasting effects on your behavior than what you are told that you should do, even if it is you telling *yourself* what you should or should not do.

Remember that the conditioning created by your past addictive behaviors has set up permanent neurological pathways in your brain. Since these pathways may never be erased, recovery consists of setting up new pathways. New pathways that affect behavior cannot be learned without their being rewarded or reinforced. It is essential, therefore, that whenever you feel like indulging in the addictive behavior, you *force* yourself to choose an alternative, healthful behavior *that provides pleasure*. Each time you make such a choice, because of the way the brain works, it will become progressively easier to make that same choice again.

In a moment we will ask you to do Exercise 2-1, where you will be asked to visualize what life would be like years from now both with and without your habit having been active in the interim. Which scenario looks better? If it is the scenario *with* the addictive behavior, then throw this book away. If it is the other, then ponder how much better off your life situation would be. Now, turn to the end of this chapter and do Exercise 2-1.

Next, work on the realization that *you* are the one who started yourself on the path to your addiction. This also means that you are the one who has to force a change in that path. Yes, we said "force." So far, the urges to engage in the addictive behavior are still there, and in full force. If you are to alter a behavior that influences you in a major way, you are literally going to have to force change upon your behavior, especially in the face of urges.

Let's add to your reasons to want to change your addictive habit! Turn to the end of the chapter and do Exercise 2-2 now.

One of the greatest difficulties in taking the traditional Step 2 of the Anonymous groups is finding and accepting a "Higher Power." In our plan, you need to find and accept a rational attitude about your life. If you are a very skeptical person, how can you come to believe that rational, logical, realistic thinking can restore you to sanity? In other words, how do you know that substituting acceptance of reality for shoulding and demanding can help you be a happier person and help you recover? Only, of course, by giving it a solid, sincere, genuine trial. Each of the following chapters will help you do this. The effects of thinking rationally can be immediate. It does not necessarily take years of insight into your unconscious conflicts and repressed memories to alleviate depression and to stop using cocaine. But, because the impulse to think depressing thoughts, or the impulse to use cocaine keep recurring, you have to continue, many times a day, to deliberately think rationally. Only after doing this over and over, and experiencing the rewards of doing so many times, will the rational thinking become as automatic as the irrational thinking of your chain of addictive conditioned reactions. Then, you will genuinely begin to recover from your addiction. So give it lots of effort, persevere, and refuse to give up. Eventually you will believe—not out of blind faith, but because of the evidence of the efficacy of doing this.

Because we talk often in this book about beliefs, we want to point out that beliefs come in a variety of intensities. At the weakest end of the intensity scale there is *superficial agreement*. At the strongest end of the intensity scale there is what we refer to as *conviction*. When a good friend tells you a hard-to-believe story, such as an excuse for why he didn't come to your birthday party, you might just barely believe him, not really knowing whether his excuse is true or not. Because he is a good friend, you give him the benefit of the doubt and pass it off. This is superficial agreement. On the other end of the scale, for example, is the belief that "if I walk into a brick wall, I know that I won't be able to go through it." This is a conviction.

We have seen many addicts who, while superficially agreeing with us as to what would be better for them, were not really convinced that what we say is true. This lack of conviction almost inevitably led to relapse. Thus, the degree of belief you have that the recovery attitudes will lead to your success in recovery is crucial. As you work through the program, try to monitor your degree of belief in what you are working on. If you find yourself being skeptical, try to determine what is causing your doubts. Frequently, skepticism about recovery is actually a ploy that your addictive mind is generating in order to keep you addicted. Do you find yourself thinking, for example, "I'm not sure that my habit is all that bad" or "How do I know that I'll really be happier if I stop my habit?" If you can't resolve these doubts on your own, talk them over with others who have experienced a goodly amount of time in recovery.

Our short version of the second step is:

Rational thinking can make me sane.

In order to shore up your rational thinking about reality and a rational attitude toward reality, complete Exercises 2-3 and 2-4 now, before going on to Chapter 3.

Chapter 2 Exercises

What follows is a toolbox of techniques that you can use to help yourself change. The alternative to living in reality is to live in either fantasy or oblivion. These alternatives, however pleasant they may be in the short run, do not provide long-term pleasure. An optimal degree of pleasure, for the longest possible period of time, is the goal of rational thinking and living.

↫ Exercise 2-1 ↫

To prove that you live in the here-and-now, real world, rather than fantasy or oblivion, we invite you to consider the long-term positive results of an addiction-free life. Picture yourself one year from now, three years from now, ten years from now. Compare YOUR OWN images of what your life will be like, both addiction-free and with the current problem. Do this frequently! The idea here is to strengthen your wishful thinking, to engender a desire, and to reinforce how much you want to change the addictive behavior. The number of times you do this per day is a probable indicator of your initial motivation to change.

↫ Exercise 2-2 ↫

Calculate the costs of maintaining your current addictive problem. What does it now cost you per day, week, month, year? What could you save in other benefits: social, financial, sexual, security? Write out how much your habit actually costs you per year, both in dollars and in hours of time wasted. Now write out—including dollars and hours—other activities and uses to which you could apply this money and time. If you were thinking sanely, you would use your time and money to enhance or create benefits. It is only when you deny the effects of wasting your time and/or your money on your addiction, whatever it may be, that you squander your resources in a self-destructive way.

ᓬᑭ *Exercise 2-3* ᓬᑭ

Here are some examples of rational ideas that can help improve the quality of your life.

1. I can be happier without my addictive habit than with it.
2. My addiction costs me more than it is worth.
3. I can give up my addiction.

Now, write at least ten more sane statements that can serve as your rational guidelines. You will add to this list as you continue to work your way through this recovery program, so keep this list handy, especially for the next exercise.

ᓬᑭ *Exercise 2-4* ᓬᑭ

For each one of the ideas that you have just written, write down your degree of belief on a scale of 0 to 3, as follows:

0 = I do not at all, or never think or believe this

1 = I slightly, or sometimes think or believe this

2 = I strongly, or frequently think or believe this

3 = I have a conviction, or always think or believe this

As you continue working this program, keep trying to strengthen your degree of belief in each of the rational ideas that you have written. Periodically return to this list to reassess your degree of belief in these guidelines. Where your beliefs are weak, try to understand why you are resisting believing in ideas that you have already decided are valid and realistic.

Chapter Three

Accept Reality

Step 3—*I shall let rational thinking help me.*

For comparison, the traditional Alcoholics Anonymous version of Step 3 is:

> Made a decision to turn our will and our lives over
> to the care of God *as we understood Him.*

Typically, the traditional Step 3 is very difficult for addicted persons to understand and to apply to their lives. Hopefully, the rational version of this step is easier to understand and to use for your recovery, although it will still require a great deal of thought and hard work. Another way to state this step is: *I decided to accept and act upon reality.* We mean by this only that *I shall let rationality (realistic thinking) help me.* This means that you will decide, each day, to follow the guidance that a rational attitude about reality provides you.

We left out the words "care of God as we understood Him" because of their implication of the existence of a supernatural superior, sentient, caring being. The sense meant to be retained is NOT that *I am turning my will and my life over to somebody else*, but rather that *I will let reality guide my thinking*. In order to make sure that you are thinking realistically and rationally, it is often helpful to seek expert advice. Thus, I will take seriously the advice and counsel of those whom I believe to think more rationally than I do, or know more than I do about some particular things. For example, I do not turn my will and my life over to my physician to run as she or he wishes, but I will take her or his counsel seriously, and will try to mold my behavior more in conformance with that advice. Do Exercise 3-1 now.

Our short version of this step is:

I accept reality on reality's terms.

This step contradicts the irrational idea that:

If it feels good, do it!

In order to clarify the benefits of following instructions instead of trying to do it *your way*, try Exercise 3-1 now.

The third step challenges what traditional twelve-step followers have labeled "self-will run riot," and "King Baby attitudes." "Self-will run riot" is pretty much what Albert Ellis, the founder of Rational Emotive Behavior Therapy (REBT), refers to as short-range hedonism. This is the childish, irrational tendency to do whatever feels best right now rather than whatever will lead to the greatest amount of pleasure over the longest period of time. The antidote to this tendency is to develop long-range hedonism. This often involves doing something that will be less immediately pleasurable (such as reading instruction manuals) in order to get better or more pleasurable results later.

King Baby attitudes involve grandiose ideas of superiority, such as "I am better than they are," "I can do things no one else can do," "I deserve anything I want," and so forth. Such attitudes obviously lead easily to frustration, since the rest of the world is not likely to believe in my superiority and therefore give me whatever I want whenever I want it. Humility (not "humiliation") is the antidote to this irra-tionality. Humility is simply acceptance of ourselves as ordinary people with faults, failures, imperfections and weaknesses just like everyone else.

In this rational version of the twelve-step program, then, the traditional concept of spirituality translates largely into "I am not God." If you realize that you are not God, then you have less resis-tance to following the advice of those more experienced and knowl-edgeable than you are. You will also not believe that you can escape the negative consequences of your addictive behavior. You will be able to accept that you are not invulnerable or impervious and that you can be hurt by your own arrogant and impulsive behavior. Before reading any further, turn to the end of the chapter and com-plete Exercise 3-2.

A journey of a thousand miles begins with one step. Get started on your recovery program even though you might not yet believe that it will work. You have nothing to lose but your addiction. After all, addictions are expensive in many ways, but recovery is cheap. Don't be discouraged if the journey is three steps forward and two steps back. Everybody makes mistakes. Progress in any endeavor is never smooth sailing. Don't just talk the talk—walk the walk, even if you are not yet convinced that you will get there. Too many clichés in this paragraph? Do you know why? Because many people, wiser than we are, discovered these principles long before we did. Just because you heard it before doesn't mean that it's wrong. At any rate don't just believe us. Do the exercises, and see whether they work for you. It's your will, your decision, and certainly, it's your life. Don't turn those things over to us, but do let us give you guidance based upon our experience with thousands of addicts with all kinds of addictions. The gambler can enjoy a basketball game without betting on it. The nonselectively promiscuous sex addict can learn to feel fulfilled with one mate. The alcoholic can learn to enjoy life without getting drunk. We know that. We've seen it. You can do it too.

The following story illustrates something about the intensity of belief, as well as the importance of following the guidance that a more experienced person can provide.

Once upon a time, Professor Wilson, an anthropologist, visited a primitive tribe, many miles from any civilized territory. This tribe lived in an area that was mostly quicksand. Therefore, they had to test the ground in front of them before firmly placing a foot down in order to take the next step. Because this habit was taught to them since they first were learning to walk, they were all firmly convinced that the ground before them could give way at any moment, and that the way in which they learned to walk was the only way to walk, and was essential to survival.

One day, the natives were surprised to see a man fall out of a big bird that flew high in the sky without flapping its wings. After he fell for a minute, a big white puff of cloth appeared over him, and he gently fell into their village, where he ended up sitting on the top of a tree. They helped him down from the tree, after taking a very long time to get to it, because they had to walk so slowly and cautiously. Then they had to pull Dr. Wilson out of some quicksand, into which he had almost immediately stepped. They all laughed when they discovered that they had to teach this grown man how to walk properly!

Professor Wilson showed them many things that, to them, were miraculous. The sun that came out of a tube (a flashlight); voices that came out of a box, with nobody inside of the box (a radio); and fire that came from the end of a short stick (matches). These, and many other things of which he told them—especially the airplane, which they had never seen or dreamt of before—caused them to agree that he had knowledge of a world that was very different from theirs.

He became very close to one of the natives. He asked the elders of the tribe whether he could show him this world, first-hand. They agreed, and he took him, first via helicopter, and then in the big bird, an airplane, to New York. The native was somewhat afraid to get into the helicopter and, later, the airplane, but having faith in Dr. Wilson, was eventually persuaded to do so. He could tell that these incredible objects were solid, and was not afraid that he would fall through their floors. Between the helicopter and the airplane, the native walked in his usual halting step-by-tested-step fashion. Dr. Wilson said nothing about it at that point, even though they were on a tarmac, because the journey between the helicopter and the airplane was so short.

When they landed in New York, the native gasped in horror when seeing that Dr. Wilson was no longer walking properly after leaving the airplane, and shouted at him to stop, as he would surely fall into the sand. Dr. Wilson assured him that there was no sand here, so he could walk with very little attention, care, or caution, and the native could do the same. He encouraged the native to simply step on the solid ground as he did. The native, however, proceeded to walk in his customary, cautious manner. Dr. Wilson said, "After all of the things that I've shown you, why don't you believe me when I tell you that the ground is perfectly solid and safe?"

The native said, "Well, I do believe you, but I'm still afraid. I've seen too many of my friends taken by the quicksand when they were not careful enough."

So Dr. Wilson said, "Then you don't really, thoroughly, believe me, even though you know that I have never lied to you before. Why don't you take a single step without testing the ground first?"

The native, trying to convince himself that Dr. Wilson was telling the truth, summoned all of his courage and took the first step. With that success registering in his mind, he took a second step. The third step was not quite as difficult for him. Bit by bit, the intensity of his belief in Dr. Wilson's honesty and the solidity of the ground in front of him grew until his belief became a conviction, and he was soon walking as rapidly as the other New Yorkers around him.

Now complete Exercise 3-3 before moving on to Chapter 4.

Chapter 3 Exercises

↜ *Exercise 3-1* ↝

Purchase, or borrow from a friend, a complex digital watch. Try setting the time, date, alarm, chronograph, and other features the
watch has *without the instructions*. Give yourself a half hour to do
this. Now, do it by following the instructions that came with the
watch. Alternatively, if you have a computer, try running a new
program without, and then with, the instructions. Or, try putting
together a complex jigsaw puzzle, first without looking at the picture and then while looking at the picture. Compare the ease with
which these things were accomplished with the guides to your
actions. Congratulations! You have just done a mini-version of the
third step.

↜ *Exercise 3-2* ↝

We want you to make two lists now.

First, think back to ten times when you did something to bring
yourself pleasure instead of using that time to prepare yourself for
something important. For example: Did you ever go to a movie or a
concert when you had an important test to take in school the next
day? Did you ever watch a television program instead of going to bed
at what you consider to be "on time"? Did you ever stop for a beer
with the gang and get so drunk that you wound up having an argument with your spouse or lover instead of making love with him or
her? Did you ever spend so much money on drugs, gambling, or lux-
uries that you had to borrow money to pay the rent?

Please list these recollections for yourself. The purpose is to
challenge the irrational belief that it is okay to do whatever you feel

like at the moment without regard to the future negative consequences. That belief is one of the core elements of denial.

Second, think back to ten times when you did prepare ahead of
time to maximize long-range gains. Did you study hard every day,
weeks before an exam, in order to get a good grade in a course? Did
you forgo a late-night movie in order to go to bed and thus wake
refreshed and ready to go to work on time? Did you say "No" to a few
beers with the gang in order to have a pleasant evening with your
family? Did you save money each payday so that you could not only
pay the rent on time, but have enough money left over to take a
vacation?

Please list these recollections for yourself. The purpose is to
demonstrate that if you follow rational guidelines for your life,
which may not be immediately enjoyable, the long-term results are
worth the effort.

ᴧ   Exercise 3-3   ᴧ

Write down your conclusions of what you learned from the story
about Dr. Wilson and the native. Think about how to apply this
learning to your own situation, and answer the following:

1. Do you tend to ignore the advice of people more experienced
    than you?

2. Do you often try to do things before reading the instructions?

3. Do you resent others telling you what to do?

4. Do you get upset when you suffer typical negative consequences
    of indulging your habit (hangovers, weight gain, loss of money,
    etc.)?

5. Do you remain cynical and suspicious about scientific information that shows that your habits are harmful?

6. Are you afraid to give up your habit in spite of knowing people who are happy for having done so?

Any "true" or "yes" answers to these questions indicate a resistance to accepting reality or believing in the obvious. If you find that you are being resistant on one or more of these points, discuss the issues with someone you trust, and keep challenging your resistance.

Chapter Four

Take a Look at Yourself

Step 4—*I shall make a searching and fearless
inventory of my past decisions and actions.*

For comparison, here is the traditional Alcoholics Anonymous
version:

> Made a searching and fearless
> moral inventory of ourselves.

This program's version of Step 4 means that you will take stock of
your past behaviors, the decisions you have made, and the beliefs
underlying them. The traditional version of Step 4 refers to it as a
"moral inventory." The moral principle underlying this program and
the traditional twelve-step program is the concept of *enlightened self-
interest*. Enlightened self-interest means putting one's self first without needlessly harming others, and helping others in order to help
oneself. Note that the outcome of working this step is not meant to

be self-condemnation, guilt, or shame, but rather *unconditional self-acceptance*. This means acceptance of yourself as a fallible human being in spite of your past behaviors, no matter how bad some of them may have been. Through this kind of examination, you will have the material available for you to decide which beliefs and behaviors to eliminate, and which ones to keep and improve upon. This will enable you to learn from your own past experiences. This will enable you to change.

Our rational short version is:

I'll take a good, hard look at myself.

This is a step during which *you* had best do a lot of work! It consists mostly of the exercises provided at the end of the chapter.

This step challenges the irrational idea that:

My past decisions and behavior
define forever who I am.

The implication of this irrational idea is that if I have done seriously bad things, I am a bad person who can never change and ought to be severely punished for the rest of my life. In order to genuinely look at and evaluate my past decisions and behaviors, it would be necessary for me to overcome this belief. The fact is, many of my decisions and behaviors have been inappropriate, but certainly not all of them, or I would be dead by now. Nobody is perfect, and all of us have made serious mistakes. The fear of facing these mistakes is based upon the act of totally condemning yourself. It is important for each of us to learn to face up to our mistakes honestly so that we may learn from them how not to make the same mistakes again and again. In order to do this, you had best learn to evaluate your thoughts and actions rather than your total being. Separating your *total self* from specific things that you have thought, felt, and done is essential in order to be able to change.

The first exercise is an examination of your beliefs, specifically your irrational beliefs. Read further before doing that exercise. Irrational beliefs are:

- Illogical. (If you don't like me, nobody will ever like me.)
- Unrealistic. (I never do anything right.)
- Unprovable. (Everyone would react the same way.)
- Overgeneralizations. (If I fail this test I'm totally stupid.)
- Catastrophizing. (It's terrible that my salary increase was not what I thought it would be.)
- Dichotomous. (I am either totally good or totally bad.)
- Demanding. (Things should, must, have to, ought to go my way and I need them to.)
- Perfectionistic. (It would be terrible if I got less than I want on my exam, or in my paycheck, or in acknowledgment.)

What you believe—the way you think about your life—leads you to make decisions about how to act and causes you to feel one way or the other about how life turns out. The ABC Theory of Albert Ellis's Rational Emotive Behavior Therapy says that what you believe or think about your life situations directly causes how you feel and act toward those situations. What happens to you does not directly cause your emotions or behavior; your attitude toward these events causes your reactions.

The ABC Theory

To help you remember the ABC Theory, look at it this way. **A** is the event, stimulus, or trigger. **B** is your belief, thought, or attitude about A. **C** is the emotional/behavioral consequence of your thinking B to yourself. It is deceptively easy to think that A, not B, causes C. If a man threatens your life in order to take your money, you would most likely say that his putting a knife at your throat (A) was why you became frightened and gave him your wallet (C).

In fact, you became frightened and gave him your wallet (C) because you thought to yourself, "I don't want to die!"(B). If at point B you had irrationally been thinking, "Life stinks and I wish someone would kill me," you might have, at point C, felt relieved and thus refused to give him the wallet. In that case, rational thinking would probably have cost you your money but maybe saved your life, while irrational thinking would most likely have cost you both! Yes, under *most* circumstances, it is irrational to give up on life altogether. In Chapter 7 we will explain the ABC Theory further, and show you how to utilize it to solve your emotional and addictive problems.

In Exercise 4-1, be as honest as possible to discover some of the more important beliefs that are diminishing the potential quality of your life. *Do Exercise 4-1 now*, before reading further.

The second exercise will reveal another aspect of your thinking, the decisions that follow from your rational or irrational thinking. In our robbery example, the irrational thinking led to relief and withholding the wallet while rational thinking led to realistic fear and giving up the wallet. As you write out Exercise 4-2, think about how your good and bad decisions have followed from your rational or irrational beliefs. If you have made bad decisions but have acknowledged few irrational beliefs, perhaps you had best do Exercise 4-1 again, more honestly and courageously! *Now complete Exercise 4-2* before reading further. Take as much time as you really need. Be thoughtful, insightful, and ruthlessly honest with yourself.

In the process of recovery, it is important to recognize that your character flaws and emotional disturbances promote your addictions, and that your addictions cause emotional disturbances and affect your personality. For example, very shy people might use alcohol to loosen up socially; depressed people may use stimulants such as cocaine or methamphetamine to be able to work; victims of severe trauma might use heroin, gamble, shop, or become sexually promiscuous in order to forget the past, or at least not to care about it for a while. It goes the other way, too: years of addictive behavior make people depressed and crazy, and can seriously warp their personalities. Most addicts, for example, become chronic liars. Many also become chronically depressed as a result of losing their money, jobs, families, friends, and often everything they ever valued in life. It is therefore important for you to make a sincere, honest assessment of your emotional states, behaviors, and personality traits. Exercises 4-3 to 4-5 are designed to help you do that.

Exercise 4-3 is an exploration of the emotional effects of your rational and irrational thoughts and decisions revealed in Exercises 4-1 and 4-2. As you answer the questions in this exercise, try to see how your feelings come directly from your attitudes and decisions. While doing Exercise 4-3, do not be ashamed to admit to yourself that you became too angry, jealous, anxious, depressed, and so forth. The more honest you are at this point, the easier it will be to change and ultimately to be a happier, less addicted person. Now, before reading further, do Exercise 4-3 and answer the emotions questions.

The fourth exercise is just listing your actions according to whether you believe they have been good or bad for you (first) and others (second). The best act is one that helps you and helps someone else. Examples would include: cooking a superb meal for your family or at a restaurant for which customers are happy to pay a good price; making love with someone who loves you; teaching your child a new skill in a way that is fun for you both. The second best kind of act is one that helps you and no one else. Examples would include: watching a movie by yourself on TV; masturbating; eating a good meal you prepared for yourself. The third best is helping somebody else without benefit to yourself. Examples include: giving money to charity; baby-sitting when you would rather be fishing; helping a blind person to cross the street safely.

The worst kind of act is one that hurts yourself and another. Examples include: getting into a physical fight at a bar over political differences; mugging someone to get money to gamble with or to buy drugs; cheating on exams rather than studying in a course graded on a curve. Of course, there is much ambiguity here, and there are in-between categories. Helping yourself, for example, while hurting someone else would generally fall in between the third and fourth categories. An example would be robbing somebody to get food in order not to starve. Giving money to charity might rank higher if it helps your tax situation, lower if it seriously deprives you of important things. Eating a meal you prepared for yourself probably helped the grocer feed his or her family. But you are the judge in this case. Be as honest as you can in ranking your behaviors. The result should be a rough guide for you as to how best to act and not act. Again, observe the relationship between your beliefs and decisions (B) on the one hand and your emotions and actions (C) on the other. Complete Exercise 4-4 now.

The fifth exercise in the chapter is a listing of your good and bad personality/moral traits. A trait is a relatively stable and enduring collection of beliefs, decisions, feelings, and actions that, over many, many situations, characterize you. For example, we say about John that he is *dishonest and can't be trusted*. This means that, possibly more often than not, he believes it is okay to lie, steal, or cheat; that he decides to do those things; that he feels little regret over (or even enjoys) such behavior; and that he often acts that way. We say that Sam, on the other hand, is *hard working*. This means that he believes that life's rewards are proportional to the effort expended; that he decides every day to do his best; that he feels good about putting in a solid day's work; and, of course, that he usually works hard to get things done. Review the first four exercises now for cues as to your basic personality traits as they are right now, and then complete Exercise 4-5. The traits upon which we ask you to rate yourself in this exercise are the ten broad personality traits that decades of research by psychologists (e.g., Krug 1980 and Cattell, Eber, and Tatsuoka 1970) have determined to be the primary components of human personality. Do not be afraid to judge your negative traits honestly—remember, the ultimate purpose of Step 4 is to help you realize which traits you would like to change or diminish, and traits which you will wish to retain or enhance.

The sixth and final exercise in this chapter will be to begin keeping a "rational notebook." This will be an ongoing daily activity for you, as it will enhance the likelihood of your success in overcoming emotional difficulties in your life as well as your addictive behaviors. Look at Exercise 4-6 now, and begin your rational notebook. Additionally, before proceeding to Chapter 5, continue your work on Exercise 1-5.

Chapter 4 Exercises

๛ *Exercise 4-1* ๛

Rate each of the following twenty ideas or beliefs according to the following scale:

> 0 = I do not at all, or never think or believe this
>
> 1 = I slightly, or sometimes think or believe this
>
> 2 = I strongly, or frequently think or believe this
>
> 3 = I have a conviction, or always think or believe this

1. Everybody who is important to me **has to** love, like, approve of, or respect me.

2. I **must** be superior or perfect in whatever I do.

3. People who do bad things are bad people and **must** be punished.

4. It's terrible and catastrophic when things go wrong.

5. My feelings are caused by what happens in my life or by other people.

6. If something might go wrong, I **have to** get upset and worry about it.

7. It's easier to avoid than to face life's difficulties.

8. I **can't** overcome the effects of all the bad things that happen to me.

9. There's a perfect solution to every problem and it **has to** be found.

10. Happiness comes from not having important or responsible things to do.

11. Others **have to** help me because I can't do very much on my own.

12. I **can't help** but get upset over other people's problems.

13. The world **should be** fair.

14. I **can't** control or change my emotions.

15. I **need** my (addictive) habit in order to be happy and handle life's problems.

16. I **should** be able to control my addiction absolutely.

17. There is nobody or no set of guidelines more sensible than I am that can help me.

18. I would **never** let anyone else make decisions for me.

19. I do not think it is good for me to examine my faults.

20. I would **never** tell anyone else all of my "sins."

Total your scores for all twenty statements.

If you scored	*You are probably*
0 to 10	Very rational
11 to 20	Relatively rational
21 to 30	"Normally" neurotic
31 to 40	Rather neurotic
41 to 50	Distinctly irrational
51 to 60	In serious trouble!

ॐ **Exercise 4-2** ॐ

Write a list of the ten best decisions you have ever made in your life. Examples might include: "I decided to go to college." "I decided to become an engineer." "I decided to stop smoking." "I decided to see a rational psychotherapist." "I decided to learn to play the guitar."

Then write a list of the ten worst decisions you ever made in your life. For example, you might write: "I decided to drop out of high school." "I decided to marry Joan because I got her pregnant." "I decided to use cocaine because I thought it was not addictive." "I decided to go to a concert instead of studying before finals in college." "I decided to have unprotected sex with a promiscuous person."

♈ Exercise 4-3 ♈

Review your work from Exercises 4-1 and 4-2 now. Think over the last month. Your rational and irrational ideas and decisions have led to various emotional reactions. How often and how strongly have you experienced the following emotions during the last month of your life?

Rational Emotions	*Irrational Emotions*
Irritation	Rage
Sadness	Depression
Concern	Anxiety
Remorse	Guilt
Disappointment	Shame
Frustration	Anger
Caring	Jealousy
Satisfaction	Pride
Happiness	Ecstasy
Regretfulness	Resentment
Enthusiasm	Desperation
Desire	Neediness
Love	Dependence
Preference	Apathy
Hopefulness	Blind faith

Rate yourself using this scale:

    0 = only weakly or almost never
    1 = mildly or sometimes
    2 = moderately or often
    3 = strongly or almost always

Remember that irrational beliefs are illogical, unrealistic, and self-defeating. The emotions that irrational beliefs lead to are exaggerated, are inappropriate for the situation, or lead to unnecessarily harmful behavior toward oneself or to others.

Total the scores you gave to the rational emotions. Next, total the scores you gave to your irrational emotions. Finally, divide the second total by the first total, and write the result in your notebook. Your score will range between 0 and 1. The closer to 0, the more rational you were this past month. Repeat this exercise every month to see whether your level of rationality is increasing. **Warning!** If you are still using a chemical substance to cover up or escape from bad feelings, your scores might be meaningless. In the early months of recovery, you might find that you become excessively upset or irritable quite often because you are missing indulgence in your habit. As you continue to recover, however, your score will likely decrease continually. The ideally rational person, if one existed, would attain a score of 0. Consider a score of 0.3 or less as very good, and a score of 0.7 as meaning that you'd better work a lot harder on the exercises in this book, and try to get outside help to chill out.

↫ Exercise 4-4 ↬

Write a list of the ten specific best things that you have done in your life. Next, write a list of the ten specific worst things that you have done in your life.

In order to be specific, do not say, for example, "I used drugs." Say, "I spent $500 on cocaine last Christmas and couldn't buy my kids any presents." Don't say, "I have helped people." Say, "I helped John get a job."

ॐ   *Exercise 4-5*   ॐ

First, reviewing carefully the last four exercises, in order to try to get a good, objective sense of *who you generally have been as a person*, rate yourself on the following personality traits. Second, rate yourself on these same traits *as you would prefer to be*. Use the following rating scale to rate each of the characteristics listed:

0 = only weakly or almost never

1 = mildly or sometimes

2 = moderately or often

3 = strongly or almost always

Superstitious and different from others (vs. realistic and ordinary)

Depressed (vs. enjoying life)

Uninhibited (vs. inhibited)

Poorly controlled (vs. overly controlled)

Anxious (vs. serene)

Passive (vs. active)

Introverted (vs. extraverted)

Dependent/group-oriented (vs. independent/rebellious)

Sensitive (vs. tough)

Illogical (vs. logical)

In each case, if your self-rating differs by more than one point from your preferred rating, then make a checklist of five things that you can do to help change yourself to be more like your own personal ideal. Perseverance in following up on completing each item on your checklist will bring gratifying results.

∿ Exercise 4-6 ∿

Begin keeping a rational notebook. We recommend that you use the same notebook in which you are doing the other exercises for this recovery program. Further, we recommend that you start your rational notebook on the last page of the notebook and work your way forward. This is because it is hard to tell how many pages it will require, and it is best to keep all of your work in one place, when possible.

In order to keep a rational notebook, every morning write one (or just a few) realistic, logical sentences that can help you cope with reality, restore your sanity, and reduce your addictive behaviors. Some examples include: "I can regain control of my life. I can learn to think more rationally. I do not have to be afraid to face my mistakes. I have a right to make mistakes. I do not have to be perfect. I will not should on myself today. No matter what I have done, I am not a worthless person. I accept myself as I am. I accept reality on reality's terms. I can give up my addictive behavior. My addiction is my enemy, not my friend. I want to stop hurting myself and those I care about. I am not in charge of the world. I don't have to be the best person in the world. I don't have to have all of the answers. I can help others while helping myself. If it doesn't keep me alive, I won't demand it. I don't need to feel good all of the time. Gambling is likely to cost me more money than it brings me. Overeating won't help my figure, my health, or my sex life. Smoking crack is like shooting myself in the head. Promiscuity can kill me. The Surgeon

General says that cigarettes are dangerous to my health. Heroin does not help to solve my life problems. Getting drunk doesn't win friends or help me drive. Anger doesn't change the people or things I am angry at. Depression doesn't make me happy. Guilt and shame can cause me to relapse. I can stand discomfort when I don't indulge my habit. I don't have to give in to urges to indulge my habit."

If you can't think of a rational sentence to put into your rational notebook, think back to yesterday or the day before and determine what irrational thoughts you had. Then try to write statements that contradict the irrationalities. If you still cannot think of a rational sentence to write, then pick one of the examples we've given here that applies to you or your situation, and that you truly believe would help you if you really believed it. Each day, read *all* of the rational sentences that you have already written. Also, don't be afraid to repeat yourself or to write the same thing in several different ways. This is a learning process, and bit by bit, the sane ideas that you write in this notebook will sink in and become a part of your automatic thinking.

Chapter Five

Tell Someone Else About Yourself

Step 5—*I shall admit to myself and to another human being the exact nature of my wrongs.*

The traditional Alcoholics Anonymous Step 5 is:

> Admitted to God, to ourselves, and to another
> human being the exact nature of our wrongs.

If you have been doing all of the exercises in the previous chapters, you have already admitted to yourself the things that you have done wrong in the past, based upon bad decisions that you have made, emotional problems that you might have, and character flaws or some negative personality traits. This has probably been very difficult work for you, perhaps even emotionally painful. However, a problem cannot be solved unless you know what it is. If you have been denying your problems, there is no way to solve them. We have also found, however, that simply admitting your problems without accepting yourself in spite of them can lead to more problems, such as guilt and shame. We have all known people, for example, who constantly beat themselves over the head about their bad behavior, but who never change their behavior. This is not the goal of self-admission. Therefore, our use of the term "admit" implies an accepting, non-self-condemning attitude.

We have also found that the act of telling your admissions of wrongdoing to another person or persons greatly reduces relapses into denial. Otherwise, if you keep your admission to yourself, you are leaving the door open for your addictive mind to say, "Well, maybe I was being too negative or harsh on myself," thus engendering yet more denial. For example, let's say that you admit the following to your best friend: "At your birthday party, I got so drunk that when I got home I had a big fight with my wife about it, and I punched her so hard I loosened her front teeth." This admission would then prevent you from telling others—or even convincing yourself—that you just had a mild argument with your wife and hit her by accident.

In a different scenario, let's say that you gambled away your rent money two months in a row and almost got evicted. If you admit this to someone else, you won't be able to pretend that your financial problems aren't really that bad, or that you had the situation under control right along (when in fact you had to get a loan from an aunt). It also stops you from convincing yourself that if your horses had won, it would have been a smart move after all.

Carefully choose a person to speak with about this. You would not want to talk to your physician about the problem you have with your plumbing. Likewise, you would not want to talk about your addiction with your grandmother if she knows nothing about addiction. The other person to whom to make your admissions would best be a recovering addict or a sophisticated professional who can deeply understand the thinking, motives, feelings, and behavior of an addicted person. This person had best not be someone who will be shocked or offended, or who will moralize.

"Admit" does not mean *confess*, which implies shame. Do not use the admissions of your wrongdoings to judge *yourself* in a highly negative light; rather, judge *what you have done* in a negative light. In other words, feel bad about what you have done, not about yourself. Regretting the wrongs you have done is good for you; it will motivate you not to repeat the same wrongful acts. On the other hand, if you do make yourself feel ashamed, you are even *more* likely to repeat your addictive behaviors in order to get a high that masks the shame.

As you can see, there is little substantive difference between the traditional and rational versions of this step. The rational step eliminates, but does not preclude, the necessity of a divine listener. Jack Trimpey, founder of Rational Recovery Systems, dislikes this step because of its "confessional" tone. The admission of fallibility, however, is essential to any therapeutic process, including recovery. This is why psychotherapists enjoy the privilege of confidentiality much like that of priests and ministers. Honesty is widely considered a *necessary* aspect of recovery, and this step encourages recovering persons to be honest with themselves and with someone else.

The short version of this step is:

I'll admit what I've done wrong.

This step challenges the irrational idea that:

I should be ashamed, embarrassed, and guilt-ridden
for what I have done in the past and should,
therefore, never let anyone else know about it.

The honesty required in this step is sometimes misunderstood as meaning total honesty with all people. Note that neither the traditional nor the rational step requires this. In fact, in the traditional

Anonymous programs, the principle of anonymity cautions you against telling everyone just for the sake of telling all. The purposes of telling at least one other person, who should be trustworthy and knowledgeable, are to get honest feedback about the thoroughness and accuracy of your fourth-step work and to keep you honest, thereby avoiding the trap of denial. One way to make this step easier, although it is never going to be easy, is to privately write or type your admissions onto paper. Then tell as much of it as you are ready for to someone you trust. Later, when you are more ready, tell more of it to that person, and continue this process of writing and admission as your recovery proceeds. Writing it out, and thus having a permanent copy in black-and-white, can also help reduce the natural tendency to minimize or deny these facts at a later time.

The primary blocks to working Step 5 are shame and guilt feelings about the serious mistakes you have made. It is better to do a partial Step 5 and proceed to Steps 6 and 7 than to spend too much time trying to perfectly complete the fifth step. Perhaps you feel ready to reveal some things but not others. Do what you can now and then use the ABCDE Method from Step 7 to help work out the shame and guilt feelings about those bad behaviors you are not ready to reveal yet. As you keep working to become more rational, you will probably return a number of times to Steps 4 and 5. That is, the less ashamed and guilt-ridden you feel about your addictive and irrational behavior, the more honest you can be with yourself and with others.

A real-life example will help clarify this process. A woman we'll call Linda was severely emotionally, physically, and sexually abused by her father and others for many years. In addition to being very emotionally disturbed, she had become irrationally dependent upon opiates, nonselective promiscuity, and abusive relationships. One of her major emotional problems, not surprisingly, was difficulty in trusting others. Her shame and guilt feelings, particularly about having abused other children as she herself had been abused, made it extremely difficult for her to be honest about her past, even with herself. In the process of therapy, she did much fourth-step work. Typically, she would write out an episode, present it to her therapist, and wait with great anxiety to see whether, after reading it, the therapist would reject her. Since, of course, her Rational Emotive Behavior therapist unconditionally accepted her each time, she would then be able to talk about and expand upon each incident. Having been honest with her therapist, she was often able to discuss these issues in either peer-group therapy or with at least selected others. She left therapy with much more acceptance of herself, which in turn allowed her to sever the destructive relationship with her father. We believe that this never would have happened had she not done her fourth- and fifth-step work so well.

Now proceed to Exercise 5-1. Remember to put your admissions in writing as Linda did.

Chapter 5 Exercise

๛ *Exercise 5-1* ๛

Choose carefully a person who fits the following qualifications:

1. Someone whose judgment you admire.
2. Someone whom you believe to be trustworthy enough to maintain your confidentiality.
3. Someone with expertise born out of an experience with a similar problem. This means either another recovering person or a professional person with proven experience in recovery from addictions.
4. Someone who will be honest and straightforward while, at the same time, unconditionally accepting of you as a total person in spite of your wrong past decisions and behaviors.

Now, having chosen that person (with his or her acceptance of the role, of course), tell him or her all of your Step 4 work which you are able to share at this time and have an honest conversation about it. Be open-minded enough to accept suggestions from this person and be willing to follow them for your own good if you find them to be reasonable.

Although there is only one exercise for this step, it may be a very difficult one for you to take, and you need to have courage and determination to do it. We believe that this part of the recovery process could be essential to your recovery, and that trying to skip it might allow you to "cop out" and find excuses later for relapsing into your addictive and self-defeating behavior.

If you find that you cannot complete the exercise for this chapter in the real situation, then it might help you to first complete it in an experimental practice, or rehearsal situation. As vividly as possible, and in complete detail, imagine telling the person you have chosen all of your Step 4 work. You might have to do this a number of times before you feel confident that you can do it in real life. This imagination exercise, by the way, has been shown to work 80 percent as effectively as actually doing the step in real life. It is called Rational Imagery Rehearsal and can be used in many other situations. It is a valuable tool to learn to use in overcoming shyness, increasing assertiveness, and so on. The key to effectiveness in using this method is the detail with which you use your imagination. Try to see, hear, feel, and even smell everything that might go on in the real situation. Imagine the situation in step-by-step detail. Remember, you can stop at any point, change your mind, and replay it the way you would like it to be, just like you would play a videotape. Then, as soon as you can, talk with the person you have chosen. Do this repeatedly until you have revealed all of your Step 4 work.

Chapter Six

Get Ready to Straighten Out Your Act

Step 6—*I am ready to have rational thinking remove my shortcomings.*

For the sake of comparison, the traditional Alcoholics Anonymous version of Step 6 is:

> Were entirely ready to have God
> remove all these defects of character.

Instead of relying on God to straighten you and your life out, the rational Step 6 means that *you* fully intend to work hard, using the tools of REBT as presented in this book, to help yourself. Even most religious people generally agree that God helps those who help themselves. *You* are the one who ultimately makes all of your decisions, no matter who or what you might have blamed in the past. *You* decide what *you* choose to believe and what *you* choose to do.

To the traditional twelve-step follower, this step can seem deceptively easy. Stated in the traditional way, what believer would not say, "Oh great! God, make me perfect. Then, I won't have to do anything myself." This, however, is either the traditional nor the rational interpretation of this step.

This step challenges the irrational idea that:

> I'll never be able to change enough
> to be happy without my bad habits.

The fear of change is perhaps one of humankind's most pervasive fears. Each of us has a part that wants everything to stay the same for ever and ever. Every psychotherapist has tried to work, with great difficulty, with patients who wanted to use psychotherapy or counseling to make themselves *feel* better while they continued to think and act in the same old ways. This Rational Emotive Behavior recovery program requires profound changes in your attitudes and beliefs, your manner of thinking, as well as your actions. Do not be surprised if you feel blocked at this step and think to yourself, "I can't really do this." Yes, you can! It will not be easy, but the long-term rewards will be significantly worth it.

The psychological essence of this step is that "I am willing to use sane guidelines and continuing hard work to change my thinking and behaviors for the better so as to improve the quality of my life and that of those affected by me."

The short version of the rational Step 6 is:

> I'm ready to straighten out my act.

In order to help you be honest about how ready you are for this task, answer the questions in Exercise 6-1 now.

You can take as much time as you want, but trying to rush through this program by skipping steps will yield few, if any, benefits. Please work this program one step at a time and one day at a time. You are not in a race with time or in competition with others. You are investing yourself in a lifelong program of change, which requires determination, effort, and patience. At the same time, please recognize that in some ways you might never be able to complete perfectly all of the steps. In each case, do what you are able to do now. You can always do more on any step later. No matter how often you return to an exercise in a previous step, keep proceeding through the rest of the steps. Stopping the work or skipping exercises will not get you very far. Continuing to work, at whatever pace or fashion, will keep you recovering.

In the traditional twelve-step programs, the constellation of addiction-promoting attitudes (discomfort anxiety, low frustration tolerance, and short-range hedonism) is hypothetically dealt with through reliance on a Higher Power to remove these "defects of character." In practice, it seems to us, the "A" support group is what helps the addict face the discomforts of ordinary life without reliance on the addictive behavior. When the alcoholic feels like having a drink, his or her best bet is to go to an AA meeting or call the sponsor. There, people will help talk him or her out of it. The real help comes from the group.

In our program, while there is certainly no harm in attending a support-group meeting, the real work must be done *by the individual*, using the tools presented in this program. Therefore, for you to make a permanent change in your attitudes, you need to continue to determinately and consistently challenge your own irrational thinking. In REBT, rational thinking ("I can stand not drinking," "I am strong enough to resist another cigarette," "I don't need the high," "I can function without placing a bet," etc.) is used to cope with the constellation of irrational attitudes that promote maintenance of your addiction(s).

Step 6 requires both determination and humility. *Determination* is a willingness to put up with short-term discomforts or annoyances in order to achieve long-term gains. *Humility*, remember, is *not* humiliation; it is accepting yourself as a fallible human being. Humiliation, on the other hand, is a total condemnation of one's self, based upon not being perfect.

In order to determine whether or not you understand the difference between humility (self-acceptance as an imperfect person) and humiliation (shame), do Exercise 6-2. This exercise will help you differentiate between (1) recognizing that you have faults and (2) condemning yourself as a total person for having those faults. Do Exercise 6-2 now, and then immediately follow up with Exercises 6-3 and 6-4 before going on to Chapter 7.

Chapter 6 Exercises

๛ Exercise 6-1 ๛

Record "Yes" or "No" for each statement below. For any answer of "No," go back to the relevant chapter and complete the work!

1. The negative consequences of my habit outweigh the positive consequences (see Exercises 1-1 and 1-2).

2. I am willing to put forth the effort to overcome the difficulties in beating my habit (see Exercises 1-1 and 1-2).

3. There are no changes that I am unwilling to make in order to eliminate my habit (see Exercise 1-4).

4. I have done, and am continuing to do, Exercise 2-1.

5. I have completed Exercise 2-2.

6. I have completed Exercise 3-1.

7. I have completed Exercise 3-2.

8. I am already working to reduce my score on Exercise 4-1.

9. I have at least started Exercise 5-1.

10. I am willing to learn and apply the ABCDE Method of problem analysis and solution, introduced in Chapter 4 and presented in detail in Chapter 7.

๛ Exercise 6-2 ๛

Answer each of the following statements twice. The first answer will be *how you actually respond* (react to the statements) *right now*. The second answer will be how you would respond if you *unconditionally accepted yourself* as someone who wants to improve your behavior, and, at the same time, humbly admitted [ACCEPTED THE IDEA] that absolute perfection is *not* very likely.

1. When I make a mistake in my checkbook, I feel:

    a. frustrated or annoyed at my carelessness.

    b. rotten because I think I'm hopelessly incompetent because I should have gotten it right in the first place.

2. When I forget someone's name when about to make an introduction to a friend, I feel:

    a. confused and, perhaps, apologetic.

    b. like falling through the floor, hoping never to be seen again.

3. If I accidentally ran over my neighbor's cat with my car I would feel:

    a. sorrowful about my mistake and want to try to make it up somehow.

    b. like a no-good sinner who ought to be run over myself or burn in the eternal flames of Hell.

4. If I, having decided to stop gambling, give in and buy a losing lottery ticket, I would feel:

    a. more determined than ever to resist the temptation to bet on anything.

    b. like a total fool who will never be able to resist temptation.

5. If I impulsively tried to seduce my neighbor's spouse, I would feel:

    a. very annoyed at my own behavior and sincerely try to mend the damaged relationships.

    b. try to laugh it off and have a drink, take a hit, place a bet, have sex, eat, throw up, and so on (*indulge in my habit*) in an attempt to forget about the whole thing.

6. When I cannot complete my income tax form right, I think:

    a. I'd best get the help of someone who is better at this than I am.

b. I'm a total failure. This should be simple for me to do.

7. If my spouse believes I am a "hopeless case," I think:

   a. He or she had best go to a Families Anonymous, Alanon, Naranon, Cocanon, etc., meeting!

   b. I'll never be able to stop my habit. So, why try?

When *any* of the answers are not the same the second time through as compared to the first time through, then your humiliation level is too high, and you'd best pay particular attention to the next chapter, Step 7, where we present the working guts, the *methods* of Rational Emotive Behavior. The method is more important than the theory, but both will be explored. Note that all of the "b" answers imply shame or humiliation and not humility.

ᴖ *Exercise 6-3* ᴖ

The following true-false test will help you pinpoint areas of resistance you might have to using the ABCDE Method to overcome your addictive behavior.

1. I'm afraid that I would feel awful if I gave my habit up and wouldn't be able to stand feeling so uncomfortable.

2. I'm afraid that if I give my habit up, I really couldn't enjoy myself any more.

3. I believe it really couldn't work for me because everything else I've tried has failed.

4. I believe that nothing will work for me because I'm too weak and bound to fail.

5. I'm afraid to try because if it fails, that will prove I'm a totally hopeless failure.

ᨮ *Exercise 6-4* ᨮ

For each "true" answer to the Exercise 6-3 statements, answer the following questions:

Statement 1.

    a. Would I feel totally awful, terrible, agonized, or merely very but tolerably uncomfortable?

    b. Would the discomfort last forever or would I eventually feel better?

    c. Since many others have been able to stand giving up a destructive habit, couldn't I?

Statement 2.

    a. Haven't I ever enjoyed anything other than my habit?

    b. Couldn't I learn to enjoy new things if I would try hard and long enough?

    c. Wouldn't giving up the problems caused by my addictive behavior help increase my enjoyment of life in the long run?

Statement 3.

    a. Did I really do my very best with the other methods?

    b. Isn't it possible that I have learned some things by my previous effort and am more motivated now so that, in spite of previous failures, I'm in a better position to succeed now?

    c. Isn't it possible that this method, because it is more scientific and more thorough, might work even where others have not?

Statement 4.

    a.   Haven't I ever done anything right? Write a list of a few of these things no matter how minor or trivial you consider them to be.

    b.   Can't people, with sufficient effort, strengthen themselves in many areas?

    c.   Isn't it possible to fail many times but eventually succeed?

Statement 5.

    a.   Since everyone makes mistakes when learning something new, can a failure *prove* that success is impossible?

    b.   Is it not possible that you could achieve partial success and wouldn't that prove you are *not* a total failure?

    c.   Even if you fail this time, in spite of all this work, can that prove that you won't be able to succeed at a later time after you have had more experience, maybe have learned more, and maybe are more motivated?

Chapter Seven

Straighten Out Your Act

Step 7—*I shall apply rational thinking to remove my shortcomings.*

The traditional Alcoholics Anonymous version of Step 7 is:

Humbly asked Him to remove our shortcomings.

The rational version of Step 7 is saying, "I shall work to suppress my demanding and impulsive tendencies, and give in to what I know is a *more sensible* way to live." Obviously, the rational version of this step places the burden of change on you, the individual, rather than on some individual outside of you—God or anyone else. It also, however, emphasizes the importance of open-mindedness to the opinions of others who have had more experience than you have had in dealing with the problems of addiction, either personally or professionally. Once again, we wish to remind those who do believe in God as a Higher Power of the motto, "God helps those who help themselves."

Our short version of Step 7 is:

I'll think more rationally.

This step challenges the irrational idea that:

I should have what I want when I want it.

What Is Rational Thinking?

Rational thinking is thinking that considers reality first, and considers wishes for that reality only secondarily. Demands on reality are far from being rational thinking, as are most prayers. Prayers, when they are used to ask God to do something to change your life in some way, are a cop-out for *you* doing something to help *yourself*. Most prayers, after all, are arrogant demands that God act the way *we* want Him to act. For example, "God, please let me win the lottery today!" This prayer is nothing more than playing the role of God *to* God. Spirituality is sometimes considered, by religious people, to be primarily the acceptance of the fact that we ordinary persons are not God. The "King Baby" attitude that allows us to act as if we *are* God is the antithesis of both *spirituality*, in the traditional twelve-step program, and *rationality* in this program. *Not* thinking that we are God is what we, and the traditional Anonymous programs, mean by *humility*.

In 1962 Dr. Albert Ellis published a basic work in the field of the psychology of emotions, *Reason and Emotion in Psychotherapy* (see the Reference section for a citation of the latest revised edition). In that book, and in the practice of psychotherapy that followed, the idea that adults are each individually responsible for most of the emotional feelings that they experience has been a major influence in the practice of psychotherapy today. Dr. Ellis developed the *ABC Theory of Emotions* and the *ABCDE Method of Coping*, both of which have received increasing amounts of scientific validation since their inception.

Remember from Chapter 4 that when something happens that we react to emotionally (let's call it **A**), we react to it by making an immediate, automatic judgment about it or rating of it. Let's call the process of making the judgment or rating **B**. If the judgment or rating of A is positive, this creates a good feeling about A. If the judgment or rating of A is negative, then the feeling that gets created about A will also be negative. Let's call the feeling that results from the judgment or rating **C**. So the something that happens (A) leads us to react by automatically making a judgment or rating (B), which causes a feeling (C) about A. That is $A \rightarrow B \rightarrow C$. Notice the sequence, here. A stimulates B to occur, but it does not determine what B will be. B causes C to happen. The major point, here, is that A *does not directly cause* C; that is, the events that happen in our lives (A) do *not* cause our emotional reactions (C). A judgment or rating (B) of the event (A) must occur, or *there will be no emotional reaction* (C). Epictetus, an ancient Roman philosopher, put it this way in the first century, A.D., "People are disturbed not by things, but by the views they take of them." Also, in the seventeenth century, William Shakespeare wrote, "There's nothing either good or bad, but thinking makes it so." These gentlemen's references to "the views" and to "thinking" are about B, and how it relates to feelings.

When referring to the nature of A, we said, "something happens." We want to further explain what "something happens" means. A can be something that we see, hear, smell, taste, or feel. Regarding the latter, "feel" can refer to a physical event, such as hitting our thumb with a hammer while driving a nail, and it can also be the result of a prior $A \rightarrow B \rightarrow C$ sequence, that is, another emotional feeling. A can also be an internal, physiological state, such as hunger, fatigue, a headache, or urges for certain drugs created by withdrawal from them. Further, A can be a memory of a past event. We have seen many people become markedly upset, for example, while telling us about some wrong done to them in the past. Additionally, and important for addicts, A can be a fantasy about the future. This fact can play heavily into what causes resistance to treatment and the perpetuation of denial. It is also what causes urges to perform addictive behaviors. Gambling addicts can see themselves winning a big bet and feeling ecstatic, or losing the bet and feeling upset. Heroin addicts can see themselves writhing in pain if they don't get a fix, or see themselves feeling euphoric upon snorting or injecting the heroin. In summary, A can be something inside of you or outside of you; it can be something in the past, present, or future. We will sometimes refer to A as the *activating event*.

B's are *beliefs*, attitudes, opinions, decisions, or other kinds of thoughts. The only kinds of B's of concern here are those that cause emotions and urges. Those are the ones that have an evaluative component, such as making judgments or ratings of any A. We have already discussed the differences between rational and irrational thinking. All of the time, we were really talking about B. Please refer back to Exercise 4-1 for a very incomplete list of irrational ideas (B's).

C, being the direct *consequence* of B, is an emotion or feeling, including urges to indulge in addictive behaviors. Depending upon what B is, C can be positive or negative, rational or irrational. The emotional reaction is usually intimately related to some behavior. This behavior can, in fact, be considered as part of C. Thus, your anger can include yelling or hitting or kicking. Your depression can include sitting around doing nothing useful, crying, or acting overly critical. Your urges can include indulging in your chain of addictive conditioned reactions, or, alternatively, seeking help. Loving frequently includes hugging someone. Joy frequently involves smiling or laughing. And so on. C's that come from rational B's can help you. C's that come from irrational B's typically hurt you, and possibly others. See Exercise 4-3 for a partial list of rational and irrational C's.

Here's an example:

> If the activating event, **A**, is My *car got a flat tire*.
>
> and if the thought or belief, **B**, is *This is awful! The damn thing shouldn't have gone flat!*
>
> Then **C**, the consequence, would probably be something like unrestrained anger, even tire-kicking rage.

Here, the judgmental rating applied is highly exaggerated and unrealistic. The word *awful*, like the words *horrible*, *terrible*, and *catastrophic*, implies 100 percent bad. Compared to the death of your child or a nuclear holocaust, getting a flat tire is a minor evil, certainly not awful. Thinking to yourself that it shouldn't have happened is also unreasonable in the face of the reality that the tire is already flat. For the sake of emotional and behavioral serenity, and for the sake of your recovery, remember to restrict the use of words like *should*, *must*, *need*, *ought to*, and *have to* to apply only to reality. Thus, in this instance, the tire should have gone flat, based upon the reality that it did. In other words, the tire had to go flat because of the circumstances that obviously made it flat, perhaps being punctured by a nail or a shard of glass.

Please note that there are times when the demanding, imperative concepts implied by *ought to* and *have to* are legitimately used. These are conditional statements that refer to reality. For example, before you can turn off your TV set, it *has to* have been turned on first. In order to do well in school, you *must* study. If you want to get candy out of a vending machine, you *should*, *must*, *have to*, *need to* put money into it. If, on the other hand, you don't want candy, there's no reason why you *ought to* put any money into the machine. Be very careful when using these concepts in your speaking and thinking vocabulary! Most of the time, they are used in an unreal-

istically demanding sense. Further, these concepts are what we call
"slippery," in that you may start out using them properly, but when
the conditional circumstances become frustrated, the same words
can take on their more usual demanding aspect, such as when you
put your money into a vending machine and the candy doesn't
come out. At that moment, it is very easy to think to yourself,
"Because I did what I should have to get the candy, the machine
should have done the right thing!" Here B represents demandingness, and thus is likely to make you feel upset and angry. It may lead
you to strike or shake the machine, instead of just feeling frustrated
and disappointed.

In our example, the thinking (B) about the tire having gone flat
(A), could have been *What a pain in the ass! I sure wish this hadn't
happened.* Then the emotional consequence (C) would likely have
been something more like feelings of frustration, concern, disappointment, and perhaps irritation. These kinds of feelings do not
usually give rise to inappropriate behaviors.

In the first case, B (This is *awful*! The damn thing shouldn't
have gone flat!) was irrational (illogical and unrealistic), thus causing unnecessarily distressing, exaggerated feelings. In the second
case, B (What a pain in the ass! I sure wish this hadn't happened)
consists of logical, realistic, nondemanding statements of personal
opinions about the situation. Because the opinions are largely negative in tone, the resulting feelings are also likely to be negative, but
are not likely to be exaggerated. "What a pain" certainly refers to a
degree of emotional discomfort, but does not ordinarily mean 100
percent of the agony that one could possibly feel. For instance, if
some maniacal dictator lobbed a nuclear bomb into the center of
New York City, simply saying "What a pain in the ass" would come
nowhere close to the intensity of emotion that such an event would
likely arouse. It is, however, appropriate to events such as a flat tire,
breaking a nail, or losing your wallet.

Here's another example:

If **A** is *I got caught drunk on the job and was fired.*

and if **B** is *I shouldn't have gotten caught, and they shouldn't have fired me.*

Then **C** would probably be something like feelings of shame, anger, or depression, and a strong urge to get totally smashed to the point of oblivion.

Feelings of shame are created when we rate ourselves as being inferior, worthless human beings. Feelings of depression are created when we overgeneralize that thinking; we reflect that we always have been inferior, and we predict that we will always be inferior. Thinking, "I shouldn't have gotten caught" contradicts the reality of getting caught, and it implies that I am inferior for having gotten caught ("If only I had hidden it better . . ."). When we demand that we should have acted differently, we are also putting our total selves down at the same time. The other part of the B, "they shouldn't have fired me," contradicts the reality of having already been fired and has two implications. First, it implies that life should always be "fair" or "good to me." Second, it implies that when people do things to me that I demand that they not do, they are automatically bad people, and they deserve my blame and condemnation. Blaming and condemning others makes us feel angry toward them.

On the other hand, B could have been *Getting drunk on the job was a stupid thing to do. It would have been better if I hadn't done it.* Then C would result in feelings more like regret, disappointment over having made a bad decision, and sorrow. In this case, the individual shows recognition of having made a grave error, which is good because it can provide motivation to avoid the same error in the future. Here, the feeling of sorrow is about the decision and the consequent act of drinking on the job, not about self-pity. It might also include sorrow about the consequences of the decision and the act—having to find another job. When we recognize that a single act of ours was wrong, we don't typically go on to overgeneralize this as representing our entire selves. Also, here the person accepted the reality that getting fired was a natural consequence of the inappropriate behavior, instead of condemning the boss for firing him or her. This acceptance of reality prevented a C of anger.

Now, the task is to learn how to apply the ABCDE Method to those situations in your life that result in inappropriately strong negative feelings or urges to indulge your addictive habit. As you know from your own experience, inappropriately negative feelings very frequently lead to your addictive behavior. That is why it is especially important for you to apply the ABCDE Method whenever it appears that your feelings are irrational or inconsistent with the reality of the situation. With the ABCDE Method, you learn how to convert the irrational judgments and ratings into more rational judgments and ratings.

The ABCDE Method

The ABCDE Method sounds so simple that it is too obvious for most people to see! All you have to do is keep a part of your awareness on your feelings, and let them guide you to appropriate action. For example, when you start to feel that you are getting angry at someone, *use this feeling* as a call to action. First, in order to become aware of your own thinking, ask yourself *what it is* that you are *telling yourself* (B). Tune in to that little voice at the back of your head. What is it telling you—that is, what are you demanding or insisting upon? What is A (the situation) as you understand it, and what is it that you are *specifically* thinking to yourself about A? At this point, do Exercise 7-1.

Now, we want to teach you the ABCDE method and introduce you to the concepts of **D** and **E**, which will plunge you right into

the self-treatment part of our program. **D** is your own effort to contradict B's, which are hurting you or your lifestyle. D stands for *dispute*. Disputing is questioning and challenging a value, an attitude,
or a belief that you erroneously have assumed to be true. Many of
the values, attitudes, and beliefs that we assume to be true are, in
fact, not really true! That is, we do not have proof that these beliefs
are valid, or true in the real world. Frequently, in fact, we have
much evidence that contradicts many of our long-standing values,
attitudes, and beliefs. For example, I might have, for many years,
thought that I was stupid because my father told me that I was, in
spite of the fact that I got good grades in high school and college.
Another example is that it was once thought that only Haitians
could get AIDS. Then it was thought that only homosexuals could
get AIDS. Then it was found that anyone can get AIDS. More difficult to contradict are paranoid ideas where you always make
excuses to prove your point. For example, if you believe that everybody thinks that you are ridiculous and a fool, and your proof is that
you frequently pass people on the street who are laughing, you
would naturally assume, *with no evidence whatsoever*, that they are
laughing at you.

Remember that B's are judgments and ratings, which cause emotional and behavioral reactions. Be aware that these judgments and
ratings are completely based upon your fundamental, well-learned
values, attitudes, and beliefs. You can tell when there is something
wrong with your judgments and ratings about a given situation if
they are yielding excessively intense negative emotions or urges, or
are leading to destructive behavior, such as indulging your habit.
When those consequences are occurring, the chances are that you
are thinking irrationally. Thus, when your analysis of a feeling that
you are experiencing is that the feeling is inappropriate, then you
know it is time to dispute your irrational B's.

According to *Webster's New Collegiate Dictionary*, *dispute*
means:

To contend in argument; to debate; often, to argue irritably; wrangle.

1.   To make a subject of disputation; to argue pro and con.

2.   To oppose by argument or assertion; to deny the truth or validity of.

3.   To contend about; contest.

D means to fight back at the B's (beliefs, thoughts, ideas, values, judgments, or ratings, or whatever else you tell yourself about A) that drive you to self-defeating emotions or behaviors. Literally, D means to argue with your own dearly believed and dearly beloved ideas that result in your judgments and ratings and, ultimately, in your habit and the unhappiness that results, in turn, from your addiction to anything. The process of disputing can be done entirely in your head, although we have found that it helps to dispute your irrational thinking out loud or, better yet, on paper.

What we would like to achieve in this section is to teach you to contradict untrue ideas until you are thoroughly convinced that they are untrue. Remember, those untrue ideas are what lead to irrational judgments and ratings of A. You will learn to question the roots of your own demands and to challenge thoughts, ideas, beliefs, and values that are false. In other words, we want to teach you to *dispute* your own nonsensical thinking so that your judgments and ratings become appropriate and realistic! Wonderfully, **E**, the effect of disputing false or irrational beliefs, is to feel and act better, at least to the extent that your feelings and behaviors become appropriate to the situations rather than exaggerated and out of control.

Let's go back to the example of the flat tire. The irrational belief was *This is awful ! The damn thing shouldn't have gone flat!* If this was your first thought about the problem, then an appropriate dispute or challenge could be something like this:

What's my evidence that this is truly awful and that it absolutely shouldn't have happened? There's nothing to *prove* that my situation is truly awful; I'm just arbitrarily or by habit telling myself that it's awful. It is, however, very inconvenient. There is also no reason why my tire *shouldn't* have gone flat just because I didn't want it to. The thought that I don't want it to be flat is a valid opinion which, however, reality has just denied to me.

As we noted in the discussion of the example, the irrational demand that the tire shouldn't have gone flat is nonsensical, based on the facts; no matter how hard or vehemently I demand that it not have gone flat, it is still flat. What a waste of emotional energy!

Questioning and challenging B's that make you feel bad or needy in some way will produce a more rational thought process. More specifically, the *dispute* will allow you to argue yourself out of the *demanding* stance, and into one of thinking in terms of your own *opinions* about the same situation. Recall that demands are absolutistic. Demands mean that you are placing 100 percent importance on what you are demanding. Usually, when we make demands, we are doing so because reality does not conform to our desires. We rarely demand in situations where we like or accept reality as it is. Therefore, demands are usually illogical or unrealistic. Opinions, on the other hand, vary in importance or intensity, according to conditions, and can, therefore, be logical and realistic. Even when they are not logical or realistic, they tend not to result in great emotional upheaval, for the very reason that they are moderated. I would, for example, love to be able to fly with no mechanical assistance, but I place only mild importance on this desire because I know it will never happen. It is an unrealistic desire, but it doesn't cause me great distress. Were I to *demand* the same thing, obviously I would be highly disturbed every time I thought about not being able to fly.

Look at the following examples of each of these two kinds of thinking:

Demands	Opinions
should or shouldn't	want or hope
need and need to	wish or desire
have to	prefer or like
must	it would be better if
ought to	it would be nice if

The left-hand column shows the category of thinking called *demandingness*. The right-hand column shows the better, or replacement, thinking: *opinions*. Thinking in terms of opinions will almost never drive you to the extreme emotional positions that, in turn, could easily be used as triggers for you to indulge in your habit!

It may take a while for all of this to sink in. If you are in therapy or counseling with a Rational Emotive Behavior therapist or other cognitive-behavioral therapist, ask for specific help in using the method of disputing irrational ideas. Rational Recovery groups will also help you practice this simple but difficult work. Even in traditional twelve-step groups, others will help you challenge your "King Baby attitude"—your demanding thinking.

Rational Problem Analysis

One of the most efficient ways to learn to use Rational Emotive Behavior Therapy on your addictive, emotional, and behavior problems is to use one form or another of a Rational Problem Analysis. This involves analyzing the problem in five stages. An outline for such an analysis follows.

Stage 1

Define the activating event, stimulus, or trigger. This is **A**. A is anything that you perceive or become aware of that you respond to emotionally and behaviorally. Pick a situation that is troubling you now, or has troubled you recently, to be your A. Now, write what happened to you on a piece of paper. Do this for each of the following stages, too.

Stage 2

Determine the exact nature of your irrational beliefs, ideas, thoughts, values, judgments, and ratings about A. This is called **B**. To find B, ask yourself, "What am I *telling myself* about A?" This directs you to look into your own thinking. Listen to the little voice that is constantly talking to you in the back of your mind. If you are very upset or emotionally distraught, look for whatever it is that you are demanding at the moment. If you cannot write this material down at the very moment of the distress, you can always re-create the situation in your mind later, and analyze it then.

Stage 3

Write down what you *felt* when you thought B to yourself about A, and what you actually did about it. This is called **C**, meaning the emotional and behavioral consequences. Remember that your feelings or emotional reactions are the direct result of what you thought or believed about A; they are not *caused by* A. Your behavior is caused both by B, your thoughts, and by your emotions, and is further influenced by your particular circumstances, A. *Note that it might be easiest for you to fill in Stage 3 before you do Stage 2. In some cases, it might even be easiest to determine Stage 3 before you do Stage 1.* You might know, for example, that you are *angry and yelling at people* (C) even before you recognize what you are angry about (A) or what thoughts (B) are creating the anger.

The next two stages include the work that you will do to help correct the problem you have analyzed in the first three stages. *It is not insight alone that cures the problem.* Once the problem has been defined and understood, there is plenty of hard work to do.

Stage 4

For each irrational idea or belief (B) that you listed in Stage 2, write a penetrating question and rationally answer that question. For example, if you said, "I can't be happy without drinking," then ask, "Have I ever been happy while not drinking?" or "Because other people can be happy while sober, how do I know that I can't?" Your answers might be, "There were many times, before I started drinking, that I enjoyed myself," or "Maybe, because other people do it, it is possible for me to be happy without drinking, too!"

This process is called **D**, meaning *dispute*. Disputing is *the* most critical and crucial stage of the ABCDE Method. Rational disputing consists of examining the logical and factual bases of your beliefs. Irrational beliefs are either illogical or fly in the face of fact. In addition, they tend to be self-defeating or otherwise destructive. For example, if you believe that you are totally stupid because you keep doing stupid things, this is clearly wrong. If you were totally stupid, you would be incapable of even believing that you were totally stupid, since you would not be able to think. Furthermore, no matter how many stupid things you have done, you must have done some intelligent things just in order to continue staying alive. Similarly, if you believe that you shouldn't have bet your last hundred dollars on a dog race, this is illogical and nonfactual because you already did it. While it would *have been better* not to have wasted your money that way, saying that you *should not have* done so means that you must not and could not have done so. But you did! Whatever has happened could, must, should have, and had to have happened exactly the way it did, regardless of how much you regret that fact. Make a great effort to understand this way of thinking. Keep in mind that you cannot change what has already happened. Do Exercise 7-2 at the end of this chapter now.

Stage 5

E refers to the emotional and behavioral effects of disputing irrational B's. Logically, E represents the feelings and behaviors that you would have experienced when A happened, *had you been thinking rationally at that time*. You could also say that E is the emotional and behavioral reaction that you probably would prefer to have had in response to A instead of the C that you had when thinking irrationally. If, following a dispute of an irrational idea, your feelings and behaviors have changed to more appropriate or realistic ones, then you have proved to yourself that thinking causes feelings and behaviors, and that thinking differently about something causes different feelings and behaviors relative to the same A. These new feelings are not necessarily positive or happy feelings, but they are less likely to be as devastatingly negative or destructive as what you experienced at C before, and the same would be true about the behaviors that follow from the feelings. For example, once you have stopped yourself from repeatedly telling yourself that you shouldn't have bet your last hundred dollars on a dog race, you will stop feeling guilty or like a bad person who deserves punishment. Instead, you will simply feel regretful about the resulting poverty and disappointed about your decision and the resulting behaviors, such as getting high or eating something off your diet. You might also feel, of course, determined to avoid such self-defeating feelings and behaviors in the future.

Here are two examples of ABCDE rational problem analyses of common problems. The first example is about anger.

Activating event: I bet a lot of money on a hot tip at the track, and the horse came in fourth.

Belief: That stupid nag should have won! The tipster promised it was a certain thing. He should go to Hell.

Consequence: I felt angry, screamed epithets, tore up the tickets, and then I went to the bar at the track and got drunk.

Dispute: Why *should* I have won just because this guy said so? Since this guy doesn't know everything, there's no reason why the horse *should have* won. Does my tipster have to go to Hell just because he was wrong? No. Everybody makes mistakes. From now on, I'll be more careful about whom I believe. Because this has happened to me many times before, it would be in my best self-interest to stop drinking and gambling altogether.

Effect: If I had thought D instead of B, then I would have felt disappointed and cautious. I probably would have decided that I'd had enough losses for the day, and walked away from the track. I would have felt frustrated momentarily because I was not fulfilling my urge to keep gambling. Later, I would have felt glad that I did not lose any more money, have any more temper tantrums, or get drunk.

The next example is about compulsive shopping.

Activating event: I'm alone with nothing to do, watching a home-shopping channel.

Belief: These all look like great bargains. I'd be a fool to pass up great deals like these. I couldn't be happy unless I save all of this money. I've just got to buy these things.

Consequence: I felt excited and had urges to buy almost everything advertised. I bought everything that my credit card limit would allow. Then, I felt happy until my credit card bill came. At that point I felt guilty and depressed about spending my money so foolishly.

Dispute: How would passing up great deals make me a fool? Why did I think that I had to buy all of that stuff in order to be happy? Even though it was a foolish thing to do, doing a foolish thing does not forever make me into a fool. In retrospect, it was more foolish to buy these "great deals" than it would have been to pass them up. While it is true that I would LIKE to have all of the good things I see, that doesn't *prove* that I have to have everything I want to be happy. I was happy sometimes as a child, and some of these things weren't even invented yet.

Effect: Had I thought D instead of B, I would not have bought everything they advertised. I might have felt frustrated at first, but happy later that I hadn't used up all of my credit. After that, I would have confined my TV viewing to programs that make me happy without having to spend money.

Notice that in the E's in these examples, we included looking at the immediate and long-term effects of disputing irrational B's. This highlights the difference between the effects of short-range versus long-range pleasure-seeking behaviors. This difference is especially important to understand when one is trying to overcome an addiction.

In the act of performing your addictive behavior you are, of course, going for the short-term pleasure without regard to the long-term pain that your addictive behavior creates for you. Were it not for the long-term pain, there would be no reason for you to want to stop your addictive behavior. You must, therefore, learn to remember the long-term pain before engaging in your addictive behavior. You must also practice rational thinking and behavior often enough so that the long-term gains of doing so become more of a habit than the urge to indulge your present habit. Because of the way conditioning works to form your chain of addictive conditioned reactions, whenever you deprive yourself of some addictive behavior, try to reward yourself immediately. You can either do something else pleasurable or, at least, *vividly* anticipate the long-term rewards that you will receive as a result of not indulging your habit.

Now, do at least two ABCDE problem analyses (that is, Exercise 7-3). It would be best to continue doing at least one problem analysis per day until you feel secure in your recovery. By that time, you will probably find that you are doing rational disputing throughout the day as your irrational beliefs occur, and as urges to indulge your self-defeating habit come up. Remember to use irrational feelings and inappropriate behaviors as your cues to do an ABCDE analysis for each.

Chapter 7 Exercises

ぞ   Exercise 7-1   ぞ

Review the definitions of **A**, **B**, and **C** in this chapter. Make sure that you understand the differences among A (what happens to you), B (what your judgment or rating of A is), and C (the feelings and actions that are the consequences of telling yourself B about A). If you are in therapy with a Rational Emotive Behavioral therapist and you still feel confused about what A, B, and C are, get clarification from your therapist. If you are not in therapy with an REBT therapist, go to a library or a bookstore, get *A New Guide to Rational Living* by Albert Ellis and Robert Harper (1975), and read the appropriate sections.

ぞ   Exercise 7-2   ぞ

Refer back to Exercise 4-1. For each of the twenty irrational ideas listed there, write an appropriate dispute. That is, write a question to challenge the idea, and answer that question rationally. We have already disputed each of these ideas, and our disputes are listed at the end of the exercise section of this chapter. Compare your disputes with the ones that we have written to get a general sense of whether you are on the right track. Please note that our disputes are not the only possible disputes, and you may have written equally valid ones. Don't cheat! Write your disputes before you look at ours. It is not necessary to complete this exercise all at once, or before you complete this chapter. Keep coming back to this exercise repeatedly, as it will help you refine your ability to do ABCDE analyses, *which is the heart of your recovery program.*

↭ *Exercise 7-3* ↭

Refer back to the outline of the ABCDE Method. Write out one problem analysis of an *emotional* problem you have experienced recently, such as rage, depression, anxiety, jealousy, guilt, or shame. Next, write out one problem analysis of an *addictive* problem you have experienced recently, such as drinking, abusing drugs, overeating, gambling, shopping, compulsive sexuality, and so on. Remember to do at least one problem analysis *every day*.

Irrational Ideas and Their Disputations (see Exercise 7-2)

1. Everybody who is important to me **has to** love, like, approve of, or respect me.

   Why does *everybody* who is important to me *have to* have positive feelings about me? What if only some—or none—of them did? Who says that they *have to* have certain feelings just because I'd like them to? I could still be relatively happy if only some or none of them had these feelings. There's no rule that says that they must, should, or have to feel the way I'd like them to. Even people who are important to me have no obligation to make me feel happy, because that's *my* job. There are other ways besides receiving other's love or approval that I can gain happiness.

2. I **must** be superior or perfect in whatever I do.

   Is there a cosmic law that says I must be perfect or even nearly perfect? If God or nature insisted that I be perfect, then I would be. So apparently, God and/or nature are allowing me to be fallible and imperfect like everybody else in the world. While it would be desirable for me to do certain things better than some other people, it is not possible to do everything better than anyone else in the world. If I were superior to all others in generosity, I would have to be inferior to many in accumulating wealth. If I had all of the physical traits necessary to be the best possible basketball player, then I wouldn't be able to be the best, or even a mediocre, jockey.

3. People who do bad things are bad people and **must** be punished.

   Don't most people who do bad things also do good things? Aren't some things good in the eyes of some people, and bad in the eyes of others? Can anybody be rated as being totally, 100 percent, bad? When somebody does something bad, is punishing him or her always the best or only thing to do? It would be hard to imagine anybody whose *every* act is bad. Even if most people would consider serial killers bad, and deserving of punishment, the existence of serial killers hardly justifies calling *all* people who do bad things *bad people*. Serial killers are near the extreme end of a continuum of badness, and everybody else does a combination of good and bad things throughout their lives. Even serial killers, such as Ted Bundy, did good things and had people in their lives who loved them. For many bad acts, much less heinous than serial killing, training, education, and rewarding good acts are more effective methods than punishment for helping them do better. Thus, calling everyone who does a bad thing, including myself, a bad person and prescribing punishment is a silly thing to do.

4. It's awful, terrible, and catastrophic when things go wrong.

   Does everything that goes wrong deserve a 100 percent bad rating such as awful, terrible, and catastrophic? Aren't most things that I rate this way relatively insignificant as compared to my own death or prolonged, intense pain? The rating of events as awful, terrible, and catastrophic means that these events are the worst possible things that could happen. Anything less than the worst possible outcome, thus, does not deserve these ratings. Compared to a severe hurricane in my city, the fact that my car wouldn't start this morning is a mere inconvenience. Compared to getting brain cancer, the fact that I tripped and fell down during my sister's bridal procession is a minor annoyance, no matter what my sister calls me. *All* ratings are done on a continuum, and these most negative ratings must logically be reserved for *only* the most negative events possible. Furthermore, even the very worst events that people have experienced sometimes have a positive side to them. The bombing of Hiroshima, for example, ended the war in the Pacific and saved many thousands of lives. Hurricanes often, in the long run, revitalize shorelines that would otherwise ultimately have decayed.

5. My feelings are caused by events or other people.

   Don't I have any capacity to change how I feel? Am I totally controlled by the rest of the world? Don't my attitudes affect my feelings? I must have some capacity to change how I feel because sometimes I can sit around all by myself and *think* myself into feeling bad. Therefore, I must also be able to *think* myself into feeling good, or at least differently, about things. I've read about the ABCDE method earlier, and it's all about how *I* am personally responsible for almost everything that I feel and do. So my feelings are not determined by what happens to me or by other people's opinions. The fact that I have often done things that other people didn't want me to do proves that my behavior is also not controlled by events or other people.

6. If something might go wrong, I **have to** get upset and worry about it.

   How will my worry and emotional upset prevent things from going wrong? While it may result in my taking a closer look at what might go wrong, I'll certainly make better plans if I do so while I'm cool and calm, rather than upset or distressed by worry. So, when I'm concerned about something that may go wrong, I'll calmly think about it before I decide how to handle it. Furthermore, once I have decided how to handle the situation, there's no sense even thinking about it any more until it happens. (*Disputing this idea helps challenge low frustration tolerance.*)

7. It's easier to avoid than to face life's difficulties.

   Where's the evidence that avoiding my problems leads to long-term happiness? Won't avoiding facing my problems help make them worse? If I'm out of a job, then getting drunk, shopping, gambling, or smoking something doesn't help me get work. The easy way is not always the best way to go through life. It may feel good at the moment, but it usually doesn't pay off with happiness in the long run. This doesn't mean that I should seek out the most difficult ways of accomplishing what I want in life in order to prove that I'm a good person, because that amounts to self-punishment. It does mean, though, that the easiest way is not always the best way. For example, cheating or goofing off in arithmetic in the early grades makes studying arithmetic in the later grades much more difficult, if not impossible. So studying arithmetic or almost anything else, while it may seem difficult at the moment, makes things easier in the future. (*Disputing this idea helps to challenge short-range hedonism.*)

8. I **can't** overcome the effects of the bad things that happen to me.

   Haven't I already overcome many bad things? When I was very young I used to relieve myself in my diaper and I couldn't read. I overcame those problems. There's no reason why I have to carry my past into the present, much less the future. Because I can change my feelings, I don't have to continue being upset or disturbed about things that happened to me in the past. When I am upset today about something that happened yesterday or a long time ago, I'd better remind myself that *that* event doesn't exist anymore, and the only thing that's upsetting me is the thinking that I'm now doing *about* that event. Even if something in the past has permanently lowered the quality of my life, I'd still best accept it as a part of my reality. If I continue to rate it as awful or terrible, then it will make me feel emotionally upset or distraught, for the rest of my life.

9. There are perfect solutions for my problems and they **have to** be found.

   How do I know that my problems can be perfectly solved? Why must I always find even the very best solution to problems? Won't solutions to some of my problems cause other problems? There's no way that I could know that my problems can be perfectly solved. I probably couldn't even perfectly say what all of my problems are. In some cases, it would take years before I'd know how good my solutions to some problems were; so how could I ever know in advance? It's not likely, for example, that I could know absolutely which job or career would be the very best for me. Somewhere along the line, however, I have to take one job, and that might make it impossible for me to find out how other jobs would have worked out. Other similar examples are in the selection of a wife or husband or lover, and the question of how many children is the right number.

10. Happiness comes from not having important or responsible things to do.

    Doesn't it feel especially good to carry out an important responsibility, even when I'm only partly done with it? Is life supposed to be a constant vacation? While it can be enjoyable, at times, not to have any responsibilities, most people get a great deal of gratification from taking on responsibilities at work and in their personal lives. Many people, even after they retire and are on "permanent vacation," still get much of their gratification from the responsible things they did in the past, such as raising children or being successful at work. In addition, many retired people deliberately continue to take on new responsibilities, including volunteer work and baby-sitting their grandchildren. In other words, permanent vacations become boring sooner or later, and boredom is bad for addicts of any kind, like me.

11. Others **have to** help me because I can't do very much on my own.

How will I know what I can or can't do on my own without trying? Who will make others help me just because I want help? I'd better stop copping out and depending upon others to solve some of my problems or do things for me. If that were a good way to think, then all of my problems would already be solved, and I wouldn't have to do anything myself. I'm the only one who can do certain things for me. If my current problem is that I'm hungry, no one can eat for me to take my hunger away. Experts and recovering people can tell me how to recover from my addiction, but they can't recover for me; I have to do the necessary work myself.

12. I **can't help** but get upset over other people's problems.

Why *must* I upset myself when others have problems? Human beings, as social animals, tend to feel the way other people around them are feeling. That's not always a good idea. If everybody in my family is angry and arguing with each other I, of course, might tend to get pulled into the battle also, but I can choose not to do so. That's what the ABCDE method is all about: that choice. If all of my friends are panicking about the stock market, that doesn't mean that I *have to* think that there's anything to panic about, even if I own stocks. Getting too emotionally or behaviorally involved in the problems of others can provide me with the stimulus or trigger that could engage my chain of addictive conditioned reactions, thus bringing me a problem of my own. I'll remember that misery loves company, and so does addiction.

13. The world **should be** fair.

Why should the world be more fair to me than to others? Isn't what's fair for one person often unfair for another? This is yet another way of striving for perfection, which only rarely seems to exist in this world. Much legislation, in recent years, has made it clear that in trying to be fair to previously vocationally disadvantaged people in order to provide them with economic opportunities, a new unfairness was created. Quota systems were established that were then unfair to some other people. Making public transportation fair for the physically disabled necessarily inconveniences other riders. What "fair" usually means to us is what's best for us. But there's no reason why the whole world *has to* comply with my demands for what is best for me.

14. I **can't** control or change my emotions.

Don't I already do things to change how I feel? The point of most of my behavior is to change how I feel. When I'm hungry, I eat. When I'm cold, I turn up the heat or seek warmth. When I feel an urge, I get high. I can, obviously, change my emotions. Further, using the ABCDE method, I can elect not to overreact, emotionally and behaviorally, to many things. Fortunately, if I use the ABCDE method to change my emotions, it's not addictive in a negative sense, although it can develop into a nice habit.

15. I **need** my (addictive) habit in order to be happy and handle life's problems.

Wasn't I ever happy when I wasn't "high"? Before I became addicted there were many moments of happiness or even joy. Probably, part of my addictive problem is that I've relied on the addiction *instead of* other methods to alleviate my misery and make me happy. If I take responsibility for my own feelings, then I won't feel like I need my addiction anymore. (*Disputing this idea helps challenge discomfort anxiety.*)

16. I **should** be able to control my addiction absolutely.

    Wouldn't absolute control mean that I'm not addicted? I can't think of many things that I can control absolutely. I've already tried to control my addiction by engaging in it less often, engaging in it at different times, engaging in it with different people. I have even tried switching from one habit to another. Because I haven't been able to control it even moderately, much less absolutely, I guess I can't control it. The only good way to control it is by giving it up. (*See Step 1.*)

17. There is no one more sensible than I am who can help me.

    Isn't there anyone in the world who knows more about certain things than I do? Aren't there people who are more experienced, informed, or intelligent about certain things than I am? There are many areas in which there are others who are more experienced than I am. Recovering from my addiction is certainly one of those areas. (*See Step 2.*)

18. I must **never** let anyone else make decisions for me.

    Why shouldn't I let certain experts make some decisions for me? It makes sense to me to take advice from people who have already accomplished what I am trying to do, or from someone who helped others accomplish the same goal that I want to reach. It also makes sense for me to act on the knowledge of what is better for me in the long run than to continue to do what feels good in the short run. (*See Step 3.*)

19. I couldn't stand to examine my faults.

    Why can't I accept myself as a fallible person? Would I die if I discovered that I'm not perfect? If I were infallible I would be

God. If there is a God, I doubt that he or she would be addicted. Even though I'll never be able to make myself perfect or godlike, I can reduce some of my all-too-human faults if I acknowledge that I have them in the first place. I need not condemn myself for having these faults and feel humiliated or like dying simply because I have the completely human problem of not being perfect. *(See Step 4.)*

20. I must **never** tell anyone else any of my "sins."

    Why not? Should I feel so ashamed that I have to hide my faults? If I stubbornly refuse to put myself down for being a fallible human being, then I will have no problem with revealing my faults ("sins") to a knowledgeable and trustworthy person. If I do that, I might even get some good advice. *(See Step 5.)*

Chapter Eight

Get Ready to Make Amends

Step 8—*I shall make a list of the persons I have harmed, and determine to make amends to them.*

For the sake of comparison, here is the traditional Alcoholics Anonymous twelve-step version of Step 8:

> Made a list of all persons we had harmed,
> and became willing to make amends to them all.

The idea behind both Step 8 and Step 9 is to rid yourself of some of the baggage that you are currently carrying around with you. This refers to those things from your own history that, when you reflect upon them, trigger you into feeling emotions that then can and might serve as triggers for you to indulge in your habit. Thinking of them in the same irrational way as you always did will, of course, bring the same inappropriate emotional result(s) they always did. The trick, here, is to learn different and better ways to think about the old circumstances.

Making amends means compensating for loss or harm that you have caused to other people. As you recover from your addiction, you may very well want to see some of the people whom you have avoided due to your addictive behavior. This may include such people as those you owe money to; those you avoided because you didn't want them to know about your addiction; those who didn't share your addiction and, therefore, weren't fun to be with; those for whom you had responsibilities that you avoided or couldn't handle. This may also include some people who care about you, or used to care about you, but whom you avoided because you felt ashamed or guilty while in their presence. Then, there are those whom you stayed with and whom you were using in some way. Maybe they gave you a place to live, fed you, "lent" you money that you never repaid. Maybe they made you feel like you were "normal" or had a "normal" social life. Maybe they were your parents, your spouse, or your children—people who refused to abandon their relationship with you because they love you. Then, there is that class of people who aided and abetted your addiction, as you did theirs. As you recover, you might find that some of them are worth going back to, as you might be able to help them (see Step 12).

Among the ways that addicts frequently hurt people, some of which you may have already written about in your work on Step 4, are the following:

Started arguments with people you love or who loved you in order to have an excuse to indulge your habit.

Started arguments or fights with people you didn't know or hardly knew while you were high.

Borrowed money, under false pretenses, to indulge your habit.

Acted obnoxiously in public while you were high.

Had an automobile accident, or other kind of accident, because you were high.

Stole money so that you could indulge your habit.

Lied about where you had been to your friends, family, or boss.

Missed work because of your habit.

Failed to keep promises to do things with or for somebody so that you could indulge your habit.

Exposed your children to bad habits that might lead them to believe such habits are normal adult behavior.

Had inappropriate sexual relationships because you were high.

Performed your job poorly because you were high or too tired due to indulging your habit or because you were distracted by thinking about your habit.

Encouraged or helped somebody else to become addicted because you wanted a companion.

Caused medical problems to yourself that loved ones worry about.

It is our hope that this list, though incomplete, helps jog the memory bank where you store your guilts, embarrassments, and shames. Think very carefully about what you have done, not only to others, but to yourself as well.

A primary purpose of this step is to help you relieve yourself of some guilt feelings that may, some day, serve as conscious or unconscious triggers for relapse. One good way for you to get rid of guilt feelings is to act more responsibly. The willingness to make amends often implies swallowing your irrational pride. Irrational pride is a defense against feelings of guilt and shame. It is the mistaken belief that "I am so superior that nothing I do is wrong, even if others think it is." Another way to try to avoid guilt and shame is to blame your poor behavior on other people. So it is possible that you carry around resentments toward those people, which, in turn, result in more excuses for you to carry out your habit. The willingness to make amends, therefore, also means giving up the resentments you tend to carry around with you, which are sustained by irrational thinking. When you learn to accept yourself as a fallible human being, you will no longer need these protections (feelings of superiority and resentment) against guilt and shame.

There is an old saying that says when you pick up one end of a stick, you are also picking up the other end. When irrational pride or resentments are at one end of the stick, the other end is its opposite, namely total worthlessness and lack of any esteem. The idea of swallowing irrational pride and letting go of resentments, then, means not to pick up the stick, or more often, to put it down. As long as you hang on to pride and resentment, you are also setting yourself up to eventually feel guilt and shame. Sooner or later the day will come when the results of your habit will be so blatantly destructive that you can no longer feel proud of yourself or blame your habit on other persons (see Step 1). As we have said before, you had best not think of yourself as a superior or perfect being, and you had best not think or believe that *other people* are responsible for *your* bad behavior. The only way to do this is to learn to believe that *you have a right* to be the fallible human being that, of necessity, you are.

When it comes to guilt, the usual paradigm is to start off with the premise, "I didn't do what I should have done," or "I did something I shouldn't have done." Then you use this irrationally demanding idea to prove to yourself, and to anyone else who will listen to you, that you are a *bad* person who ought to be punished, at least emotionally if not in reality. This means you need to learn to take a realistic view of the incidents during which you think you have hurt others. Not only do you need to list their names, but you also need to learn how to protect yourself from putting yourself down as a bad person as a result of your actions. Logically, you would only put your *self* down if you now take a negative view of your entire self as a totally bad person. Instead, apply a negative rating just to your bad behavior. Regretting your bad behavior is quite rational. But condemning your *total* self is completely irrational and is the cause of guilt feelings. Recognize that feeling guilty because of total self-condemnation doesn't help improve your behavior. Instead, most often it puts you in a position of thinking that you can't improve your behavior. After all, if you are totally bad, how can you do good things, too? Thus, guilt feelings only cause you to punish yourself or make you feel that you deserve punishment; they don't truly motivate you to change your behavior!

Furthermore, in most of the situations where you have hurt others, you were functioning under the influence of the addiction, whatever it may have been at the time. To blame yourself, as a total person, for the results of your addictive behavior is to blame yourself for having inadvertently learned a chain of conditioned reactions. Thus, you are not a bad person trying to become a good person. You are an ordinary, fallible person trying to learn an alternative chain of conditioned reactions. It is important, however, in the process of this new learning—and therefore recovering—to take responsibility for the bad behavior caused by your addiction. Making amends to those you have hurt is a way to begin to take responsibility for what you and your addiction have done. As long as you make yourself feel guilty, ashamed, or embarrassed about how you have hurt others, you will find it doubly difficult to face some of these people and make amends. Sometimes, amends do not necessarily have to be direct, however. There is more about this in the next chapter.

Our short version of Step 8 is:

I'll list those I've hurt.

This step challenges the irrational idea that:

> Because I can't change what I did to others in the past,
> I must always feel guilty and ashamed
> over these bad acts of mine
> and cannot possibly face those whom I've hurt.

Now, do Exercise 8-1. Put your name first on the list of people you have hurt! When you have done Exercise 8-1, do Exercise 8-2, and then proceed to Chapter 9.

Chapter 8 Exercises

➳ *Exercise 8-1* ➳

Write a list of the people you have harmed as a result of anything you have ever done in your life that, when you think about it, makes you feel guilty or ashamed. Include, for each person, the specific things that you did that you believe had hurt them.

While much of this harm may have resulted from your addictive behavior, you had best also include incidents that occurred prior to the addiction. Your irrational feelings about some of these things may have contributed to the development of your addiction in the first place, whether you recognize it or not. In order to get a jump-start on this task, review what you wrote out as Exercises 4-2 and 4-4.

➳ *Exercise 8-2* ➳

For each person you have listed, write about how willing you are to make amends now, directly to that person. After each person's name, write a few words about why making amends would be a good idea, and a number from 0 to 4, as follows:

0 = It would be dangerous to me or would further hurt or harm that person if I try to make amends.

1 = I am just not thinking rationally enough yet.

2 = With a moderate amount of work I think I can find a way to do it if the circumstances were just right.

3 = With just a little bit of work I'll be ready to do it soon.

4 = I am ready now and intend to contact them.

Chapter Nine

Make Amends

Step 9—*I shall make amends, wherever possible, except when doing so would injure someone.*

The traditional Alcoholics Anonymous twelve-step version of Step 9 is:

> Made direct amends to such people wherever possible, except when to do so would injure them or others.

Our short version of Step 9 is:

> I'll try to make it up to them.

This step challenges the irrational idea that:

> There's nothing I can do to make those I've hurt, or myself, feel better, so there's no sense to even try it.

The people to whom you make amends includes yourself, of course, as well as others whom you have hurt. Sometimes the best way to make amends to those closest to you is simply to replace your addictive behavior with normal, ordinary activities. This is, obviously, also the best way to make amends to yourself. Learn to *enjoy* ordinary life without having to indulge in a destructive habit. Spending time with those whom you have neglected is often more important to them than apologizing for the neglect. This is especially true for young children, who are less concerned about past behavior than they are about how we treat them now. For adults, or for children who are old enough to ask questions about previous inattention, apologies are appropriate, as are answers to their questions as they arise. Your answers would best be geared to their age and level of understanding.

Some other examples of making amends follow:

Where you have borrowed money in order to indulge your habit, pay it back, or make arrangements to do so as rapidly as possible. Strongly consider paying interest on the amount due, especially if the loan was made a long time ago.

If you have stolen money or goods in order to indulge your habit, return the money or the cost of what was stolen (not the amount that you sold or pawned it for, but rather the replacement cost that your victim would have to have paid). In cases where your victim might want to take legal action if you returned goods or money to them in person, it may be wiser to make the return anonymously. Remember that the purpose of making amends is to make up for what you have done, not to seek punishment.

In those instances where you have lost friends because your addictive behavior turned them off or because you neglected them so you could more easily indulge your habit, try to reestablish the relationships. No matter which reason was the basis for the loss, apologies are appropriate, along with an expression of your gratitude for the relationship that they had provided to you in the past.

If you have missed work because of your habit—whether you went elsewhere to indulge, had withdrawal effects such as hangovers, or were genuinely ill from smoking, drinking, substance abuse, or bad diet—make amends by volunteering to work extra hours with no compensation, if your employer allows it.

Sometimes indirect amends are better than direct amends. For example, it might be better for you to go out of your way to bring the grandchildren to see their eighty-year-old grandmother than to shock her with the news that, a year ago, you stole $100 from her purse to place a bet. Sometimes, what people don't know doesn't hurt them as much as if they knew it. You are now ready to do the exercises for Chapter 9.

Chapter 9 Exercises

∽ *Exercise 9-1* ∽

Return to the list of the way that addicts hurt people in Chapter 8 and to the list that you made for that chapter's exercises. Write out a way that seems sensible to you to make amends in each of those situations.

∽ *Exercise 9-2* ∽

Refer to what you have written in Exercise 8-1, and to whomever you gave a rating of 4 in Exercise 8-2. Contact them and make direct amends. Take as much time as you need to carry this out. It need not all be done at the same time.

∽ *Exercise 9-3* ∽

Once you have completed Exercise 9-2, for each person to whom you gave a rating of 1, 2, or 3, write out an ABCDE problem analysis of your fear of making amends, or resistance to doing so. Then, determine whether you can then go ahead and make amends, whether direct or indirect. If you still have trouble, vigorously and vividly imagine yourself doing so. The process of Rational Imagery Rehearsal often results in the ability to go ahead and do the thing you are imagining. It is crucial, in using this Rational Rehearsal method, to imagine the situation in step-by-step, vivid detail. If, after this, you are still not ready to make amends, discuss this problem with your therapist, sponsor, self-help group, or someone whose advice you respect.

Chapter Ten

Continue to Look at Yourself

Step 10—*I shall continue to take my inventory, and when I act wrongly, promptly admit it.*

For comparison, the traditional Alcoholics Anonymous twelve-step version of Step 10 is:

> Continued to take personal inventory
> and when we were wrong promptly admitted it.

Do this step so that you can continue the work you started in Steps 4, 5, 8, and 9. This step summarizes most of what the traditional twelve-steppers refer to as the *working* steps, and is the key to *recovery* as opposed to just *abstinence*.

Our short version of Step 10 is:

> I'll keep looking at myself and admit my faults.

This step challenges the irrational idea that:

> Now that I've done all of this work to recover,
> I should be able to relax and simply enjoy my life.

This irrational idea does not take into consideration the idea that no human being is perfect, and that no matter how much work you have already done to better yourself, you are still not perfect. You will thus continue to make wrong decisions and behave poorly on an almost daily basis like most other people. While it may be true that as you become more reality-based in your decision-making processes and the behaviors that follow from those decisions, you will merely be *less* prone to making mistakes, either substantive or social, you will likely continue to make mistakes. The challenge is not to let these ordinary human mistakes trigger your chain of addictive conditioned reactions, thus leading you to your old modes of coping (habitual thinking, feeling, and behaving), and increasing your chances of relapse. Therefore you had best, on a continuing, lifelong basis, take care of those things that you do that engender guilt, shame, embarrassment, or lower your self-esteem.

The powerful conditioning of your psychophysiological reactions (such as urges and emotions) and behavior caused by your addiction(s) has left permanent neurological traces in your brain. This chain of addictive conditioned reactions cannot be erased by philosophical and behavioral changes. But *continued* efforts to change, especially when the changes provide rewards and fulfillment, can eventually produce an alternative chain of conditioned reactions that is as strong as or stronger than the addictive one. This process, however, requires much determination, repetition, and experience of the consequent rewards and pleasures in order to overcome the power of the addiction. Thus, the addictive behavior must *continually* be challenged and replaced. There are no easy, one-shot, magical solutions. Constant difficult but rewarding work is the *only* rational solution. At this point, complete Exercise 10-1.

Self-Revelations

If you have read up to this point without doing most of the exercises in the preceding chapters, this section is especially for you. There are a number of reasons that people don't do the work that would help them change. Taking your personal inventory might reveal some or all of the following.

Discomfort Anxiety

The fear of feeling bad, or what Ellis and Velten (1992) call *discomfort anxiety*, will hinder almost any addicted person from giving up his or her compulsive habit. You might, for example, believe that it would be terrible or awful to miss indulging your smoking, overeating, drinking, gambling, sexual, methamphetamine, heroin, or cocaine habit. If so, remember the saying "No pain, no gain!" It might very well *be* painful, uncomfortable, inconvenient, or intensely frustrating to stop your habit or to do some of the rational twelve-step exercises. But the *long-term* results will be well worth the *short-term* bad or uncomfortable feelings. They may be bad, but they are not terrible, horrible, catastrophic, or intolerable! Think about getting a flu shot, for example. While you might have a stinging feeling in your arm for a second or two, but this fleeting discomfort is certainly worth preventing two or three weeks of misery with the flu. The same is true here: Isn't it worth experiencing some short-term discomforts in the present in order to avoid the greater amount of long-term negative consequences due to continuing your addictive habit?

Low Frustration Tolerance

Impatience, or *low frustration tolerance*, might have led you to try to skip to the end of this program to find the magic answer that will painlessly, effortlessly, and immediately solve all of your problems. The bad news is that you have to work, and work hard, in order to defeat addictive habits or any other neurotic behavior, for that matter. Furthermore, you have to keep working—hence Step 10. The good news is that "It works if you work it."

Short-range Hedonism

Perhaps your reluctance to having done the exercises as prescribed is a result of a philosophy of *short-range hedonism*—your tendency to go for the immediate pleasure of the moment, rather than to consider the long-term consequences of your decisions. Short-range hedonism is one of the main causes of procrastination. If you tend to do something that is immediately pleasurable, instead of something that takes continued effort and is less immediately pleasurable, then, of course, you put off doing the more effortful, less pleasurable task. In the business of trying to recover, this tendency becomes especially destructive, because there are no deadlines that force you to do anything on time. With sufficient procrastination, you could make it so that you would require more than your entire lifetime before you finish doing what we have prescribed in this book. Some good it would do you then! The only way to challenge your short-range hedonistic procrastination is to *force yourself* to do things that you know are in your best self-interest, every single day. You will probably find that doing such work *each day* gives you a feeling of satisfaction that will reinforce your taking responsibility for yourself. If you don't find this to be the case, then periodically reinforce (reward) yourself in some way for doing the work in a timely manner. This means doing something, other than indulging your habit, that you find pleasurable. This will reverse your usual sequence. Usually, you do what's easy and fun first, and then you eventually do the hard stuff. We're suggesting that you turn that around. Do the hard stuff first, and *then* do the easy stuff. For example, first finish reading this chapter before watching the television program that you enjoy.

Perfectionism

Perfectionism, especially in the form of your fear of making mistakes or of failing to do the exercises properly, could be another important reason that you have not done some of the exercises in this program. Please remember that it is not possible to learn *anything* without the chance of making mistakes. If an exercise seems too difficult, try it anyhow. Doing it incorrectly will not *mean*, and thus ought not serve as proof to you, that you are a total idiot or a failure, or that you can never recover. It might mean that you need help from someone who is further along than you in the process of what you are trying to achieve, or has more expertise than you do in that area. It may, alternatively, simply mean that you need to try some more, or try harder. "If at first you don't succeed, try, try, again" is a pretty good motto, in our view. There is no such thing as *total* human perfection, no such thing as a totally perfectly recovering person, and, certainly, no such thing as a totally rational person. It is vitally important, in the process of recovery, to try to accept yourself as an ordinary, fallible person who has made, and will continue to make, mistakes—even very big, bad, hairy ones. Perfectionism stems from making irrational demands of yourself. It can, therefore, easily lead to feelings of guilt, shame, and embarrassment, and will make you miserable, but not perfect.

Self-Condemnation

Feelings of *shame, guilt,* and *embarrassment,* which stem from *total self-condemnation,* make you fearful of facing yourself. On the other hand, feelings of regret and remorse over specific acts, which stem from a rationally negative evaluation of your irrational thinking and behavior, allow you to face your wrong decisions and behaviors. Facing your wrong decisions and behaviors, with acceptance of yourself as a fallible human being, diminishes the irrational emotions of shame and guilt. AA espouses the *disease* concept of addiction and calls it "cunning and baffling." That concept helps diminish the feelings of shame and guilt because it helps you, as an addicted person, to separate your bad behavior from your self-concept. The addictive thinking and behaviors are thus seen as symptoms of a disease. Unfortunately, because the disease can then be considered as an entity unto itself that has taken you over, this concept can then be used as an excuse to continue the addictive behavior; it implies that you cannot exert any control over it.

Referring back to Step 1, you will recall that we prefer the term "loss of control" over the term "powerless." This is why we prefer to think of addiction in terms of a chain of conditioned reactions instead of as a disease. If you prefer to consider your addiction as a disease, be sure that you do not think that you are powerless over it, and be sure that you recognize that it can be treated, like many other chronic diseases.

Jack Trimpey (1989), founder of Rational Recovery Systems, Inc. refers to the *Beast* who, so to speak, sits inside the addict's head and provides the irrational justifications for continuing the behavior. The beast is called "the addictive voice," which is seen as an entity unto itself, and which is not your true self, very much like the AA disease concept of addiction. Again, this helps you separate yourself from the things that you are guilty or ashamed about and only temporarily helps you feel better. Some people say, "The devil made me do it!" This concept, of course, removes responsibility for the addictive thinking and behavior from the addicted person, thus alleviating feelings of guilt and shame. Additionally, some mental health experts see addictions as multiple personality disorders (Dissociative Identity Disorders) like the famous cases of Eve and Sybil. This allows the cocaine addict who mugs someone for money to buy cocaine to say, "It wasn't the *real* me who did it; it was my cocaine personality."

All of these separations of *self* from the addiction help to alleviate shame and guilt feelings. The tenets of Rational Emotive Behavior Therapy (REBT) accept the possibility that some of these ideas might have at least some degree of usefulness. If any of them help you stop rating your *total* self rather than rating your individual thoughts, emotions, and behaviors, then those concepts might be useful in your recovery. Whether your addiction is the "devil," a "Beast" in your mind, a disease, another self, or a chain of conditioned addictive reactions (the most scientific and explanatory conception of addiction), it will take much work to recover from it, and shame and guilt feelings are more likely to cause you to relapse than to recover. In any case, recognize that *you* are still responsible for your thinking and behavior, past or present. Also recognize, though, that in spite of your responsibility, you are not a bad person, deserving of being put down or of punishment because of your addiction.

Now do Exercise 10-2. Include, in your ABCDE problem analyses, any of the five problems presented here that may apply to you. Before going on to Chapter 11, remember to continue your work on Exercises 1-5 and Exercise 4-6.

Chapter 10 Exercises

✨   *Exercise 10-1*   ✨

Review Exercise 4-1. Take the test over again now, and see whether you have improved significantly, according to your test scores. If your score this time is lower than your score last time, then you have improved. Congratulations! The size of the difference between the two scores, then, indicates the amount you have changed. See whether you have moved to a more rational category than you were in before. If any of your answers are still 1 or higher, then refer back to Exercise 7-2, and revise and expand your disputes.

✨   *Exercise 10-2*   ✨

Think of any addictive behavioral or emotional problems that you have had in the past two or three weeks. Do a rational problem analysis, using the ABCDE Method, on each one of them. In examining your B's, look for irrational ideas related to discomfort anxiety, low frustration tolerance, short-range hedonism, perfectionism, and self-condemnation in addition to other irrational modes of thinking.

Continue this exercise throughout the rest of your life. When you stop, you are very likely heading for trouble.

Chapter Eleven

Continue to Straighten Out Your Act

Step 11—*I shall seek to improve my conscious contact with reality, striving for the knowledge of what is rational and for the determination to act upon it.*

Perhaps more than any other step, this one illustrates how a rational version of the twelve-step program contrasts with the original. The traditional Alcoholics Anonymous version of Step 11 is:

> Sought through prayer and meditation to improve our conscious contact with God *as we understood Him*, praying only for knowledge of His will for us and the power to carry that out.

Without excluding any metaphysical possibility, our version is compatible with Rational Emotive Behavior Therapy (REBT) *and* illustrates the psychological aspect of the original version. More specifically, we believe that the following *substitutions* are reasonable, and are well within the frameworks of both the twelve-step program and Rational Emotive Behavior Therapy:

Substitution in New Version		Traditional Version
reality	for	*God*
what is rational	for	*His will*
determination	for	*power*

Our short version of this step is:

I'll keep learning to think and act more rationally.

This step challenges the irrational idea that:

I already know enough about how things are or should be,
and shouldn't have to learn anything more.

In this chapter, we review some of the major concepts of recovery from addictions. First, we address the bases of psychological change. Making new decisions about how you act is based upon changing your emotional feelings. Changing your emotional feelings is accomplished by changing your beliefs, and thus the way you think about your world. This is the basis of psychological change. The essence of this step is for you, the person with an addictive problem, to become more deeply convinced of the truth of the rational beliefs that will help your addictive problem. You have done much work up to this point if you have taken this program seriously. At this point, we would like to deepen your understanding of the principles of psychological change.

Among the most important of the principles of psychological change is giving up *demandingness* in all of its forms. Demands in your conscious and unconscious thinking can hurt you. They can be extremely devastating! In the English language, demandingness represents a class or style of thinking. English conceptual words that fit this category of thinking include *should, need, must, ought to, have to, got to, imperative,* and the question *"Why?"* For the latter, the question is almost never a sincere inquiry, but rather a hidden or implied demand. Thus, *"Why* did you do that?" really means, "You *shouldn't have* done that!" Further examples of implied demandingness include statements such as "We Smiths don't do that sort of thing!" and "You can't talk to your mother like that!"

The main difference between a demand and an opinion is the amount of emotionality involved in the concept as you think it. *Demands* do not know degree. That is, demandingness, by definition, is always of the very highest value or importance, thus carrying the most emotionality with it. *Opinions*, on the other hand, carry varying measures of value, concern, and importance, and so they carry varying amounts of feelings, but almost never as much as demandingness.

When you think in terms of what should, must, or needs to be, and then reality doesn't match up, the feelings you get are at or near your upper level of negative affectional (feeling) strength. You feel upset, angry, resentful, vindictive, depressed, and so forth. Your demands have not been met.

In contrast, when you think in terms of what you want, wish, or hope for (opinions), and then reality doesn't match up, the negative feelings you get vary according to the strength of your original opinion. If you just wanted it a little bit, you feel mildly frustrated or disappointed. If you wished very hard for it, you feel more frustration, disappointment, or even sadness. But none of these feelings are out of control.

The main characteristics of demands are that they are absolutistic, illogical, and unprovable. Let's say someone says something you don't like. It's not appropriate to think, "He shouldn't have said that." You can't *prove* it shouldn't have been said; it's already been said. Maybe you had hoped, wished, desired, wanted, or preferred that it not be said, but this doesn't prove or justify that what *you* wanted most, should, or needs to happen. Nor does it prove that the other person must, should, needs to, or would *ever* want to say what you want him to say! So rather than demanding what should happen, it is better to hold only an opinion about it.

To use *should* properly, let it *always* refer to **truth and/or reality.** Thus, in our example, the person *should have* said what he said— even though you abhorred hearing it at the time, and you still don't like it.

In short, we are advocating using the "should" concept mostly to refer to past events and to those described by physical laws. Using "should" for evaluation of a future act can sometimes make rational sense. If you let go of a brick and you are on planet Earth, the brick *should* fall toward the center of the Earth. As far as we know, gravity on the surface of the planet is a truth, an established fact, and not just someone's guess or personal opinion. "Should" is also appropriately used to refer to conditional realities, such as, "If you want the brick to fall, in the presence of a gravitational field, you *should* let go of it."

If, in the past, a cat scratched my cornea, this proves that the cat *should have* scratched my cornea even though it hurt me very much, and I don't like it at all, either then or now! It is an established fact of reality, however, so it *should have happened.* Up until the time that the cat scratched my eye, this fact had not been established in reality and might have been prevented if I had sight into the future. However, I did not and do not! In the more distant past, I may have considered that there was a small chance that this might indeed happen to me. My judgment *at the time* was that it was so unlikely to happen I decided not to do the work necessary to prevent it. Wrong again! Of course, it would have been better if I had prevented the cat from walking on my face in the first place, but I can't prove that I *should have.* The only thing I can justify to myself logically is that *in my opinion*, it *would have been better* if I had taken those precautions that I didn't take when it counted.

Frequently, people use the word *should* in a genuinely nondemanding sense. For example, "I should rake the lawn today, but I think I'll wait until tomorrow." In that case, the word *should* simply means "it might be better if." Unfortunately, that sort of usage very easily slips into irrational demandingness, so if it turns out that it is raining tomorrow, the same person is very likely to say, "I knew that I should have raked the lawn yesterday!" Then he feels guilty and angry at himself for having made that decision. He is no longer meaning "it would have been better"; now he is meaning "it is terrible that I didn't do it when I should have done it, and I deserve punishment." He has turned a realistic preference into a moral necessity. This is why the concept of "should" is often referred to as being "slippery," and why we advocate that you stop "shoulding on yourself."

The only things that make any sense to demand for yourself are those things that actually keep you alive such as air, water, food, sleep, and warmth. This is because the result of not having these demands met—death—is for most people worse than the consequences or side effects of making such demands in most less crucial life situations.

Addicted persons usually treat their addiction as if it were a necessity of life. Addictive substances or behaviors use the same brain systems that the necessities of life do, especially the so-called pleasure pathways. These brain systems are there, in fact, to ensure that you continue to eat and drink and that, as a species, we carry out activities that are necessary for the survival of the species. These include having sex, exercising our curiosity, caring for babies, socializing, and so forth. It is as if the addiction tricks your brain into thinking that the addiction is important to survival. Thus you *demand* that you indulge your habit. The alcoholic doesn't say he *would like* a drink; he says he *needs* a drink, and then another, and then another. The gambler doesn't think she *would enjoy* placing a bet; she thinks she *couldn't be happy* without betting, and therefore *must* place a bet, and then another, and then another. The overeater doesn't say that eating a candy bar *would be nice*; he says that it would be heavenly and that he *must* have it, and then another, and so on. Thus, as an addiction develops, preferences become demands, and that's why it is so important, during the process of recovery, to learn to challenge all of your demanding thinking.

For real psychological change, you would best give up catastrophizing and awfulizing about the negative things that do happen in life. This is so whether they just happen to you, or whether they also happen to most people over the course of their lives. Common words like *terrible, horrible, catastrophe, disaster*, and *calamity* have some of the same slipperiness that the word *should* does, even though *should* seems to be the most slippery of them all. While it might be legitimate for us to call the effects of a tornado a calamity or a disaster, we would be seriously misusing these terms to describe the dress that our aunt wore to her birthday party, or to missing making an on-time payment to the credit card company. These words are intended to refer to the *very worst* kinds of things that could possibly happen and would, therefore, best be reserved for those kinds of events. When they are used indiscriminately in the process of rating and judging (B) the happenings and events (A) in our personal lives, then our emotional and behavioral reactions (C) become much exaggerated and out of proportion with the reality to which they are being applied. Such exaggerated reactions often lead the addicted person to relapse. A life of extreme highs and lows is not recommended for addicted people.

The goal of life is not reasonably to be *perfectly* happy, but rather to feel **appropriately** about whatever circumstances surround you. This can be done *without* the abuse of chemicals, food, gambling, throwing up, having inappropriate sex, shopping, or other addictive behaviors. People become addicted to substances, behaviors, and even negative feelings in a vain attempt to make life more *perfect*. Life is inherently *imperfect*. Coming into contact with reality and rationality involves an increasingly greater acceptance of yourself, others, and external reality *as it is*, without demands for you, them, or it to be different. This is a lifelong process. Do not expect any magical or instantaneous cures. Those who promise you such—by telling you to just say "no," getting you into primal screaming, probing for deep insights into your past, telling you to just pray for recovery, making post-hypnotic suggestions not to indulge for the rest of your life, or simply rewarding your good behaviors—have oversimplified the complexity of the *real* human condition. Step 10, in the traditional and rational versions, teaches us that growth is a continual and lifelong process.

The spiritual element of Step 11 consists of the recognition of the importance of continual self-examination, as in Step 10, as well as an ongoing open-mindedness toward reality and a willingness to act upon this reality. We have more to say about spirituality in Chapter 12, but do the Chapter 11 exercises now.

Chapter 11 Exercises

✢ *Exercise 11-1* ✢

Spend some serious time reviewing everything you have done in order to overcome your addictive behavior(s) so far. Then, write a short reflection on how well you think you have progressed.

✢ *Exercise 11-2* ✢

Share the essay written for Exercise 11-1 with a confidant, your therapist, your sponsor, or a self-help group in order to get some objective feedback about how honest you are being with yourself.

✢ *Exercise 11-3* ✢

If you have gotten feedback about a lack of total honesty, read Chapter 10 again and work harder on the exercises in that chapter. If the feedback you got was very positive, then proceed to Chapter 12. If you insist upon working completely on your own, your only guide to your progress would be how much you have reduced your addictive behavior. If you have reduced your indulgence in one or more addictions, then good for you! You are making progress. If you have absolutely not indulged in one or more addictions, excellent! In either case, proceed to Chapter 12. If, however, you have not reduced *any* of your addictive behaviors to any significant extent, return to Chapter 10.

Chapter Twelve

Help Others Straighten Out Their Acts

> **Step 12**—Having an increased awareness as a result of what I have accomplished with these steps, I shall practice these principles in all of my affairs, and I will carry this message to others.

The traditional Alcoholics Anonymous version of Step 12 is:

> Having had a spiritual awakening as a result of these steps, we tried to carry this message to alcoholics, and to practice these principles in all our affairs.

It is important for all of us to further the process of social progress in whatever ways we feel will be most fruitful, and we believe such social connectedness to be a primary component of the twelve-step program's concept of *spirituality*. It is also consistent with the philosophy of *enlightened self-interest*. Again, this last step captures an essence of self-help and other-help that is well within the spirit of both the twelve-step programs and Rational Emotive Behavior Therapy (REBT). In a broader sense, *spirituality* is an accurate aware-ness of, and a sense of connectedness to, all of reality.

Many wise persons have sought for an absolute moral or ethical standard, a "Golden Rule," to be the basis of our spirituality. Implicit in the twelve-step approach is the principle of *helping others in order to help ourselves.* This might not be the perfect answer for all people, but it seems to us to be an important part of being in touch with your reality. That is, the quality of your own life depends on treating yourself and others in the best way you can. This is certainly a com-monsense idea, although not easy to accomplish. It is impossible to accomplish, obviously, as long as you maintain any serious addictive habits. Our short version of Step 12 is:

> Helping others helps me.

There is no such thing as *completing* this recovery program, as we have presented a lifelong program of recovery from your addictive behaviors. If you have, in fact, gotten this far, having completed all of the exercises in the previous eleven chapters, then *it will help your recovery* and that of others to promulgate (carry this message) to others whom you know to have problems similar to yours. This process of helping others is part of carrying out the process of enlightened self-interest, which, as we've noted, we believe to be the fundamental ethical basis of both Rational Emotive Behavior Therapy and the traditional twelve-step program.

This step challenges the idea that:

> It was hard enough for me to change my self-destructive
> habits and I still need all the help I can get.
> Therefore, there's no way that I can help others
> who may need help more than I do!

Now it is time for you to complete Exercise 12-1 for Step 12. When you are ready, try Exercise 12-2. Remember that teaching something to others is a great way to learn it.

Chapter 12 Exercises

᧣ *Exercise 12-1* ᧣

Show this book—which you have just read through and, hopefully, just worked through—to other persons whom you believe could benefit from this program. Do not make a point of hanging out with active addicts, especially when they are high or in the process of indulging their habits.

᧣ *Exercise 12-2* ᧣

Help organize groups such as Rational Recovery, Secular Organizations for Sobriety, SMART, or AAAA meetings where other addicts could benefit from this integrated, comprehensive but specific, cognitive-behavioral approach to overcoming addictive behaviors.

Chapter Thirteen

Summary of Various Program Steps

This chapter summarizes several versions of the twelve-step program.

By careful comparison of these versions, you will note that the Rational Emotive Behavioral twelve-step version has the greatest emphasis on individual responsibility for personal change. The concept of spirituality has been retained in this version, but as a philosophic and ethical position rather than as a metaphysical position. In our program, recovery depends upon changes in your attitude toward life, rather than on a higher being's good will. We do not mean by this emphasis to negate the importance of the fellowship of other recovering persons or the help of trained professionals. The aid that the recovering person can get from others is often crucial or necessary to his or her recovery. But no amount of external help, whether from peers or from God him- (or her-) self, can help you unless you change the self-defeating attitudes and behaviors that lead to and maintain your addiction.

As you read through each of these versions for each of the twelve steps, pick the version that you think will work best for you. You will probably find that whichever version you pick, the exercises we have provided in the first twelve chapters of this book will help you work that step.

Step 1

> I admit that I have lost control of my addiction
> and that my life is becoming unmanageable.

The traditional Alcoholics Anonymous statement of Step 1 is:

> We admitted we were powerless over alcohol—
> that our lives had become unmanageable.

Our short version of Step 1 is:

> I can't handle this bullshit anymore!

This step challenges the irrational idea that:

> I can do whatever I want without suffering
> any serious negative consequences.

Step 2

> I believe that a rational attitude
> about my life can restore me to sanity.

The traditional Alcoholics Anonymous version of this step is:

Came to believe that a power greater than
ourselves could restore us to sanity.

Our short version is:

Rational thinking can make me sane.

This step challenges the irrational idea that:

There is nothing that I can do to help myself
be a more sane, more happy, person.

Step 3

I shall let rational thinking help me.

The traditional Alcoholics Anonymous version is:

Made a decision to turn our will and our lives over
to the care of God *as we understood Him.*

Our short version of this step is:

I accept reality on reality's terms.

This step contradicts the irrational idea that:

If it feels good, do it!

Step 4

I shall make a searching and fearless inventory
of my past decisions and actions.

The traditional Alcoholics Anonymous twelve-step version is:

Made a searching and fearless
moral inventory of ourselves.

Our rational short version is:

I'll take a good, hard look at myself.

This step challenges the irrational idea that:

My past decisions and behaviors define forever who I am.

Step 5

I shall admit to myself and to another human being
the exact nature of my wrongs.

The traditional Alcoholics Anonymous version of Step 5 is:

Admitted to God, to ourselves, and to another
human being the exact nature of our wrongs.

The short version of this step is:

I'll admit what I've done wrong.

This step challenges the irrational idea that:

> I should be ashamed, embarrassed, and guilt-ridden
> for what I have done in the past and should,
> therefore, never let anyone else know about it.

Step 6

> I am ready to have rational thinking
> remove my shortcomings.

The traditional Alcoholics Anonymous version of Step 6 is:

> Were entirely ready to have God
> remove all these defects of character.

Our short version of the rational Step 6 is:

> I'm ready to straighten out my act.

This step challenges the irrational idea that:

> I'll never be able to change enough to be happy without my
> bad habits.

Step 7

> I shall apply rational thinking to
> remove my shortcomings.

The traditional Alcoholics Anonymous version of Step 7 is:

> Humbly asked Him to remove our shortcomings.

Our short version of Step 7 is:

> I'll think more rationally.

This step challenges the irrational idea that:

> I should have what I want when I want it.

Step 8

> I shall make a list of the persons I have harmed,
> and determine to make amends to them.

The traditional Alcoholics Anonymous twelve-step version of Step 8 is:

> Made a list of all persons we had harmed,
> and became willing to make amends to them all.

Our short version of Step 8 is:

> I'll list those I've hurt.

This step challenges the irrational idea that:

Because I can't change what I did to others in the past,
I must always feel guilty and ashamed
over these bad acts of mine
and cannot possibly face those whom I've hurt.

Step 9

I shall make amends, wherever possible,
except when doing so would injure someone.

The traditional Alcoholics Anonymous twelve-step version of Step 9 is:

Made direct amends to such people wherever possible,
except when to do so would injure them or others.

Our short version of Step 9 is:

I'll try to make it up to them.

This step challenges the irrational idea that:

There's nothing I can do to make those I've hurt, or myself,
feel better, so there is no sense even trying.

Step 10

I shall continue to take my inventory,
and when I act wrongly, promptly admit it.

The traditional Alcoholics Anonymous version of Step 10 is:

> Continued to take personal inventory
> and when we were wrong promptly admitted it.

Our short version is:

> I'll keep looking at myself and admit my faults.

This step challenges the irrational idea that:

> Now that I've done all of this work to recover,
> I should be able to relax and simply enjoy my life.

Step 11

> I shall seek to improve my conscious contact with
> reality, striving for the knowledge of what is rational
> and for the determination to act upon it.

The traditional Alcoholics Anonymous version of Step 11 is:

> Sought through prayer and meditation to improve
> our conscious contact with God *as we understood Him*,
> praying only for knowledge of His will for us
> and the power to carry that out.

Our short version of this step is:

> I'll keep learning to think and act more rationally.

This step challenges the irrational idea that:

I already know enough about how things are or should be
and shouldn't have to learn anything more.

Step 12

Having an increased awareness as a result
of what I have accomplished with these steps,
I shall practice these principles in all of my affairs,
and will carry this message to others.

The traditional Alcoholics Anonymous version of Step 12 is:

Having had a spiritual awakening as a result of these steps,
we tried to carry this message to alcoholics,
and to practice these principles in all our affairs.

Our short version of Step 12 is:

Helping others helps me.

This step challenges the irrational idea that:

It was hard enough for me to change my self-destructive habits
and I still need all the help I can get.
Therefore, there's no way that I can help others
who may need help more than I do!

Chapter Fourteen

Strategies for Multiple Addictions

Probably the majority of addicted persons suffer from multiple substance and/or behavioral dependencies. It is often unrealistic or impractical to give all of them up at once, even if that is your goal. Sometimes, it is even medically unwise to attempt this. On the other hand, it is often important to give up several of them at the same time. This chapter outlines some reasonable strategies or plans for attacking complex dependency problems.

Consider the following representative cases:

1. Julia overeats, has become dependent on prescribed tranquilizers (benzodiazepines), and is a compulsive shopper.

2. Sam freebases cocaine, drinks alcohol heavily, and smokes three packs of cigarettes daily.

3. George is homosexually promiscuous, often forgoing safe sex measures with nameless partners; abuses "poppers"; smokes marijuana; and drinks "socially."

4. Mary shoots heroin, prostitutes herself to get the money for her drug of choice, continues to get involved in a string of abusive relationships.

5. Jim gambles compulsively, drinks ten to fifteen cups of coffee per day, and rarely sees his family because he is at the office fourteen hours each day, including weekends. The underlying impetus for his gambling and workaholism is his addiction to making money.

If Julia gives up her tranquilizers, her shopping and overeating will likely increase as she tries to control her increased anxiety. Sam's stress of giving up cocaine and alcohol at the same time will make it very difficult for him to simultaneously give up cigarettes. Trying to give up all three at once can increase his chances of relapse, but stopping only one at a time can lead to a sharp increase in one of the others. George had better stop his sexual behavior immediately for health reasons, but any of the drugs he uses could lower his inhibitions and make a relapse into promiscuity easier. Mary needs to safely withdraw from heroin, but it is unlikely that she will stick with that program as long as she continues to live with the man who is currently abusing her. Jim cannot afford to work less right now because he needs the extra money to pay off his gambling debts. It is probably best for him to slowly wean himself off of caffeine because sudden withdrawal would make him too sleepy to be able to put in the time at work.

You can undoubtedly see other complications in each of these cases, and the "best" course of action is largely a judgment call. If inpatient treatment is available, more habits can be given up at the same time because the risk of relapse or an increase in one addiction when another is given up is greatly reduced. The bigger problems occur when inpatient treatment is not available, and so the following suggestions refer mostly to outpatient recovery attempts. We use the term *outpatient recovery attempts* to refer to the addict who is living at home and working as usual, but is, at the same time, going for one or another kind of help several times a week. This can include self-help groups, talking to your sponsor, or seeing some professional therapist of one ilk or another. Here are some principles to use in planning your total recovery program:

1. It is best for the addicted person to give up all addictive drugs, including alcohol, at the same time. This is because of the phenomenon of cross-addiction, which can cause a dramatic increase in the abuse of one substance when another is given up.

2. The use of alcohol, opiates, tranquilizers, or barbiturates complicates matters a great deal. These substances are both physically and psychologically addictive. Withdrawal from these substances might require medical supervision and a weaning-off period, temporarily using other addictive substances. Thus, the heroin/marijuana addict can stop using marijuana immediately (not physically addictive) or cold turkey, but might be better off substituting methadone for the heroin and then tapering off the methadone over a one- or two-month period. Similarly, the alcohol/cocaine addict can safely stop using cocaine "coldturkey," but might have to switch from alcohol to benzodiazepines and taper off those over the course of a week or two in order to prevent D.T.'s, seizures, or other severe consequences of withdrawal from severe alcohol abuse. The sleeping-pill-addicted compulsive gambler would likely do best to stop gambling altogether, but taper off the abuse of sleeping pills over a period of several weeks and with medical supervision. Cocaine is not physically addictive. The addiction is not supported by feeling physically "sick," only by feeling depressed. Only the downers (alcohol, opiates, benzodiazepines) are considered physically addictive. Interestingly, addicts who have experienced both psychologically addictive and physically addictive drugs find it harder to give up the former.

3. In general, drugs and behaviors best eliminated first are those that are:

a. most immediately medically dangerous

b. illegal

c. most costly

d. most heavily indulged in or abused

4. In general, drugs and behaviors that are already highly connected for you are best eliminated together. Common examples
of this are:

a. alcohol and promiscuity when alcohol is used to reduce
sexual inhibitions

b. alcohol and cocaine when drinking leads to cocaine use
and/or is used to mellow out the effects of the cocaine

c. coffee (caffeine) and cigarettes (nicotine) if coffee is a major
trigger for smoking

d. cocaine and gambling, if snorting or shooting or smoking
produces unrealistic grandiosity, such as, "I can't lose"

Reasonable Plans for Some Combinations

Please read all of the following combinations, even if they do not
apply to you, because something in any one of them may include a
concept that would "click" with you, perhaps making it vitally
important for your individualized recovery program.

Heroin (and/or Other Opiates) and Marijuana

Unless your opiate use is *very* light, your withdrawal should be
medically supervised. We are sure that you already know whether
you experience withdrawal symptoms; if you do, then you are not
in the *very* light category. The medical supervision would best be

administered by a board-certified addictionologist. If you can't find one, choose an internist or a psychiatrist well experienced with helping addicts go through withdrawal. With such help, there are a few options available. On an inpatient basis, there has been a fairly decent success rate for rapid medical detoxification. The speed of detoxification depends, somewhat, upon the length of use and the amounts used, but usually requires three days or more—possibly much more. There is an experimental program currently being conducted at several hospitals. It is a one-day detoxification program, wherein the addict is put to sleep via anesthesia and then given a cocktail of medications intended to rapidly strip the brain and body of the opiates. This method is controversial and is still being studied. Other methods available are methadone and cold turkey. If methadone treatment is chosen, the goal should be to rapidly taper off of the methadone. Here, again, support from a medical professional is vital. Medications to assist with the withdrawal symptoms are quite helpful in shortening the period of withdrawal from years to weeks *for those committed to recovery.*

Switch from heroin to methadone and taper off of the methadone over a period of a few months. At the same time, the marijuana can be stopped immediately since there are no serious physical withdrawal effects. However, if this seems too stressful while undergoing opiate withdrawal, you could taper off the marijuana over the same period or, if both heroin and marijuana abuse have been very heavy, begin tapering off of the marijuana on the day following your last methadone dose. Schedule your last use of marijuana for one to two months after your last use of methadone.

Be aware that the first alternative is by far the best due to the potential legal consequences of continuing to smoke marijuana. Also note that as you become more confident in your ability to give up heroin and methadone, you might develop greater confidence in your ability to give up marijuana since it is not physically addictive.

Heroin and Cocaine

This includes "speedballing," which is the combination of snorting, shooting (injecting), or smoking both of them together. Give up the cocaine cold turkey. Switch from heroin to methadone and taper off of the methadone.

Cocaine has more immediately medically dangerous side effects, such as brain, vascular, and heart damage. Its withdrawal effects are, *with medical assistance*, mostly just a few days of depression and fatigue, followed by days or weeks of hunger, as the body tries to reverse the common weight-loss effect. The medical assistance during cocaine withdrawal is because the addict is likely to be quite debilitated and experiencing intense urges, and these conditions can be medically moderated. It is not, however, physically dangerous to go cold turkey. So there is little reason to delay giving it up, other than psychological reasons (the "rush" is terrific and, thus, beloved!). This is, however, a harder combination than heroin and marijuana to give up on an outpatient basis. If at first you don't succeed, get your addicted butt to an inpatient detoxification program!

Another word about methadone. There are alternative "cocktails" of medications to reduce the withdrawal pains from heroin. These require the expertise of an addictionologist, who is a physician with a specialty in addictive drug use and treatments. Also, if you want to recover fully, avoid methadone *maintenance* programs. They can, however, be useful if **you** are *bound and determined* to leave opiates as the last addiction from which to recover. We certainly do not recommend that for most addicts. While methadone is sometimes considered in the medical community a cure for heroin addiction, our program as well as the traditional twelve-step programs generally discourage the substitution of methadone for heroin. Many methadone maintenance patients have told us that they still use heroin in order to get high. They have also told us that it is much more difficult to withdraw from methadone than it is from heroin. (Medically, it takes longer and is more difficult because it has a longer half-life.) But it is up to you!

Heroin and Alcohol

Taper off the alcohol, with benzodiazepines if medically necessary, for the first week. Simultaneously, begin your methadone program. If your alcohol use is truly "social" or "controlled," you can get off of heroin/methadone *first* while continuing to drink. If your drinking stays at less than one or two drinks daily for three months after your last methadone dose, then you might choose to experiment with lifelong, "normal" drinking, at which most alcoholics fail. If the drinking starts to increase, you had better give up the booze, too! The chances are that it will start to increase due to the cross-addiction phenomenon. Remember, you are not so much addicted to heroin or alcohol as you are to *getting high*. Giving up the irrational need to *get high* is truly the way to recover. Also, it is pretty difficult to participate in AA, NA, CA, RR, SOS, SMART, or most other self-help groups while you continue drinking!

Marijuana and Cocaine

If you cannot yet get yourself to give up both at once, give up the cocaine today and start tapering off of the marijuana over a period of one or two months. When you taper off of any drug or behavior, write out a schedule *ahead of time* and **stick to it!** If you cannot stick to the schedule, go cold turkey! Medical supervision can hasten the process, but is not an absolute necessity.

Marijuana and Alcohol

If you cannot yet get yourself to give up both at once, give up the marijuana today, and start tapering off of the alcohol over a period of one to two months. Again, when you taper off of any drug or behavior, write out a schedule, *ahead of time*, and stick to it! If you cannot stick to the schedule, medical supervision will be necessary.

Cocaine and Alcohol

Stop both now, switching from alcohol to the benzodiazepines as suggested previously. Again, if you have rated yourself as not addicted to alcohol, you can try to experiment with giving up one drug but continuing to control your use of another. If you choose that path, however, please do some Step 4 work on why you prefer that to total abstinence. Perhaps you are simply trying to find some way to continue to get high because you irrationally continue to believe that you cannot be happy without your high of choice, or that you are too weak to ever really recover.

Cocaine and Sex

You are not going to stop having sex, although a temporary pause in all sexual behavior, except, perhaps, masturbation, might give you the "window of opportunity" to stop the cocaine use. Even temporary sexual abstinence is unlikely for most people, although it is expected by most of the sex self-help groups. This is much easier to accomplish on an inpatient rather than on an outpatient basis. If you are not going into a hospital or residential treatment center, give up all of those sexual behaviors, especially nonselective promiscuity, that are connected with your cocaine abuse. At the same time, give up cocaine altogether without trying to taper off. In order to give up this dual dependency, you will also have to give up the irrational idea that you need extraordinary thrills and excitement, every time you have the impulse, in order to enjoy life. We also recommend that you substitute other kinds of excitement that you have planned ahead, such as thrilling vacations with your spouse in exotic locations, or non-sexual activities such as sky diving, skiing, motorcycle or auto racing, and so forth. You might also have to work at giving up the irrational idea that "sex should be easy and I shouldn't have to make efforts to please or seduce my partner."

Cocaine and Workaholism

Using cocaine as an energizer or stimulant that allows you to work longer hours and to work harder, too, is most common among snorters. This is a combination that, while it may work positively for you for a short while, usually ends up making your work suffer in the long term, anyway. Furthermore, if you are employed by others, you can set up, in their minds, new but unrealistic standards they can expect from you and, perhaps, others. Thus, you will first need to plan to manage your work during logical, sensible hours of the day or night. Implement this plan immediately. It might take you some time to make the necessary arrangements, but be persistent. As soon as the plans are in place, give up the cocaine. You don't need to be bright-eyed and bushy-tailed all of the time now. Plan to sleep a lot at first. Your body will likely demand it of you. If possible, it would be best to start this plan with some vacation or sick time. In counseling for this disorder, you will want to explore your irrational needs for achievement and, perhaps, a grandiose sense of responsibility and obligation.

Gambling and Alcohol

Often, veteran gamblers will use alcohol as an excuse to overbet, and in games that require some skill, to overestimate their feeling of "luck" and to overestimate their own skill. After a few ounces of alcohol, your skill suffers because your memory functioning suffers, as does your judgment in general, which can then be reflected in your estimate of your "luckiness" at the moment. Thus, ideally, you will give up both the gambling and the alcohol at the same time.

Do not allow yourself to be trapped into the delusion that if you just give up drinking, you will suddenly become a winner at gambling. Remember, your gambling is also a compulsive habit and so even if you lose less, chances are you will still lose. If you want to experiment, we suggest one year of total abstinence from both habits, and then an attempt at controlled gambling. If you choose this experiment, you had better stick to gambling games that are very dependent on skill rather than just chance. The odds in a lottery or at slot machines stay the same whether you are drunk or sober. Perhaps your chances at blackjack or poker or the options market depend much more significantly upon your skill rather than just your luck. You can take your year of abstinence to study such games and refine your skill. Our guess is that after a few months you will realize the futility of your trying to make easy money and decide to spend your energies on more fruitful pursuits.

Overeating and Alcohol

This one is fairly clear-cut! Give up the alcohol first. Alcohol has so many calories that chances are you will almost immediately begin to lose weight. The complication is that giving up alcohol may increase your desire for fattening carbohydrates. So you also need to get on a good, preferably medically prescribed, diet. Also, exercise is a very important element of recovering. Again, under medical supervision, begin a program of exercising regularly on a schedule. One thing you can do today is stock your refrigerator with fresh fruits and vegetables. Every time you have an urge to drink or snack, hit the celery, carrots, or bananas. Don't worry about how much of these you consume. You can hardly eat enough fruits and vegetables to hurt yourself.

Cigarettes and Overeating

This one is also clear-cut! First, work on the overeating. Work with your doctor and get on an approved diet regimen. After you have become comfortable, or as comfortable as you think you are going to get while on your diet, and have shown a good record of weight loss, only *then* start to work on the habit of smoking. The problem, as you probably know, is that many people who give up nicotine compensate by overeating, and thereby gain weight. Furthermore, nicotine has the effect of ever-so-slightly increasing your metabolic rate, thus burning a few calories for you every day. When the nicotine is removed from your system, we suggest that you implement a medically approved or supervised program of exercise. This will accomplish two things. First, the exercise will most likely more than make up for the nicotine-based reduction in caloric expenditure. Second, exercise has the effect of eventually raising your metabolic rate.

In addition, as in the alcohol and overeating problem, developing a fresh fruits and vegetables habit can be very helpful. Smoking and overeating are both very oral habits. Munching a carrot or crunching a celery stalk can satisfy at least some of your oral cravings. Counseling and self-help groups, as for all of these dual dependencies, can help you determine the precise irrationalities that you personally use to support these habits and therefore need to learn to challenge.

Cigarettes (Nicotine) and Coffee (Caffeine)

Having a cup of coffee and a cigarette at the same time seems to many people to be a natural and harmless thing to do. If you want to stop smoking cigarettes, however, the years of conditioning the linkage between the coffee and the cigarette can be a powerful trigger; coffee can make you crave the cigarette. Therefore, it might be best to give up coffee when you first decide that you are ready to stop smoking. Thus, strategically, first work to give up the coffee. When you have become comfortable without the coffee, *then* work on giving up the cigarettes.

Fortunately, there are many satisfying substitutes for coffee. These include chewing gum, herbal teas, noncaffeinated soft drinks, and a wide variety of fruit juices. Make sure that these are available to you before you try to stop your coffee dependence. To avoid creating a new monster, do not regularly pair smoking with any particular drink. If you fear chronic sleepiness or low energy, you might want to taper off coffee over a period of several weeks rather than go cold turkey. Your brain and your body will adjust to the lack of caffeine, and, in the long run, you will probably feel *more* energetic. Regular exercise, as it does with dieting, will help your energy level and be much healthier for you than the coffee ever could be.

There is also medical technology to help with cigarette withdrawal. Acupuncture and hypnosis have worked well for some people. There are now a series of products that infuse nicotine into the body without requiring you to smoke. They are intended to prevent the physical symptoms caused by nicotine withdrawal. These include the nicotine patch, nicotine chewing gum, nicotine nasal spray, and nicotine inhaler. The patch and the gum come in varying dosage levels of nicotine so that you can stop the behavior of smoking immediately while attempting to match your body's average level of nicotine. The nasal spray is to be used immediately upon having the urge to smoke, and may be used up to forty times per day.

These "nicotine helpers" enable you to change the behavior first, while at the same time, you slowly taper the amount of nicotine until you reach a point where stopping the use of the product yields little or none of the usual withdrawal effects that have made many people fail at their multiple attempts to stop smoking.

If you prefer not to use the patches or similar aids, you might want to use Zyban, the first orally administered prescription medication (a pill/tablet) approved by the FDA for the purpose of assisting with smoking cessation. It contains no nicotine at all. The same product has been on the shelves of pharmacies for years under a different name (Wellbutrin) and still is, having been approved for use as an antidepressant medication for many years. In order to use this method, you would take Zyban for eight to fourteen days, and then plan on quitting smoking a week or two after that time. You then continue to take the Zyban for seven to twelve weeks, or until you feel confident that you are not going to relapse into smoking. Recent clinical reports suggest that the relapse rate may be cut in half by the simultaneous use of Zyban and the nicotine patch once you have stopped using cigarettes altogether. If you do not want to use Zyban, or cannot get a prescription, then you will probably want to taper off rather than stop smoking immediately. In order to do this, you need to set a definite date when you will be cigarette-free and make sure that you stick to it. Usually, tapering down to ten cigarettes per day for four days will lower your body's craving for nicotine enough so that you can go cold turkey at that point. We recommend that you set your taper-to-quit goal to between two and four weeks.

Recent research (Cinciripini et al., 1995) has shown that merely skipping some cigarettes in order to taper down the number per day is not nearly as effective as carefully monitoring *the length of time between cigarettes* (the "inter-cigarette interval"). Once you start smoking on a given day, you smoke on a predetermined time schedule. If you stay awake for sixteen hours per day, then smoking one cigarette every hour will get you down to sixteen cigarettes per day. Then, after a week at sixteen per day, you would increase the time interval between cigarettes to one and a half hours: now you will smoke twelve cigarettes per day. After that, add fifteen minutes to the inter-cigarette interval each day or two until you are smoking at the rate of around five cigarettes per day. It is then safe to stop altogether without experiencing nicotine withdrawal symptoms. If there are any such symptoms, real or imagined, then you can use the recently available two-milligram nicotine patches for a week or two. Numerous support groups, primarily through hospitals, are available to help you go through the process of smoking cessation.

In summary, most addicts have two or more addictions. Giving up one addiction can temporarily increase your indulgence in another. In the long run, giving up the first addiction will increase your sense of self-efficacy—it will prove to you that you are strong enough to recover, and that you can be confidant of your continuing progress.

Chapter Fifteen

Program Maintenance and Relapse Prevention

This chapter is especially for those of you who have tried, and tried again, to recover from your addictive habits but have failed and relapsed right back into the same, self-defeating patterns. It is simply a summary of the tried-and-true methods, detailed in the previous chapters, which you undoubtedly were exposed to in the programs that you tried. We have also included supplementary techniques not mentioned or not stressed previously. Beginners will also benefit from this chapter as it highlights many important points of this program.

We believe that the main reason for relapse is simply that people do not follow the instructions. So here are the instructions again!

1. Work the steps.

2. Learn and practice the ABCDE Method. Use it every day—all day.

3. Go to meetings and/or group therapy several times per week.

4. Get one or more temporary sponsors as soon as possible and a therapist or counselor, if needed.

5. Meditate and/or practice relaxation at least once daily, and whenever you have an urge to indulge your habit.

6. Have fun. Reward yourself for recovery by seeking *natural* highs or ways of enjoying yourself.

7. Change people, places, and things as necessary in order to avoid excessive temptations.

8. Use medications as prescribed by a psychiatrist or addictionologist.

9. Don't use any addictive substances or engage in the addictive behaviors of your choice.

10. Keep it simple.

To further explain these instructions, we will elaborate upon each one of them.

1. *Work the steps.*

Step 1	Understand loss of control
Step 2	Take reality as authority
Step 3	Accept reality
Step 4	Take a look at yourself
Step 5	Tell someone else about yourself
Step 6	Get ready to straighten out your act
Step 7	Straighten out your act
Step 8	Get ready to make amends
Step 9	Make amends

Step 10   Continue to look at yourself

Step 11   Continue to straighten out your act

Step 12   Help others straighten out their acts

2. *Learn and practice the ABCDE Method. Use it every day—all day.*

THE THEORY

a. It is not **what happens to you** (A) that causes your **feelings and behavior** (C).

b. It is your **beliefs, attitudes, and thoughts** (B) about A that cause how you **feel and act** (C). You can change your **thinking** (B). These changes will alter how you **feel and behave** (C).

THE PRACTICE

a. Accept reality on reality's terms.

b. Use the Serenity Motto.

c. Complete a Rational Problem Analysis from start to finish.

d. Force yourself (if you have to, and you probably will have to) to *act* on your new beliefs, rather than on your feelings.

3. *Go to meetings and/or group therapy several times per week.*

It is recommended that you attend one self-help meeting or therapy group a day for the first three months of your recovery. The support and reinforcement you receive from these groups early in recovery can be invaluable! If, after three months, you feel more secure, you can begin to decrease the frequency of meetings. The most successfully recovering people we have met have, after two or three years of abstinence, tapered off to only one or two meetings per month as their "maintenance" level. They also sponsor at least one other person.

4. *Get one or more temporary sponsors as soon as possible and a therapist or counselor, if needed.*

We recommend that you *immediately* get yourself at least one temporary sponsor in each type of self-help meeting that you attend. Then, over a period of months, settle upon the one or two persons who have been the most helpful to you, and ask that they become your permanent sponsors. If you continue, after three months or so of abstinence, to experience serious emotional problems, then by all means get yourself a therapist or a counselor.

5. *Meditate and/or practice relaxation at least once daily, and whenever you have an urge to indulge your habit.*

This practice could ultimately become a valuable tool. During these periods of meditation/relaxation you learn that you can control your body in very important ways. The following two methods can be used to reduce, temporarily, the negative emotions that often lead to addictive behaviors. They also can be very effective in reducing urges to engage in your addiction of choice. These are by no means curative, which is why they are not emphasized in the first twelve chapters, but they can be of great value in recovery.

MEDITATION

Pick one word or phrase that seems comforting to you. Many people will pick words like *peace, love, harmony,* or *serenity.* Others will choose short phrases like "God loves me," "I accept myself," "Nothing is terrible," or "I'm okay." In order to meditate, simply repeat your chosen word or phrase over and over again. Try not to let any other thoughts enter into your mind during your meditation time. If other thoughts intrude, redirect your thoughts back to your selected word or phrase. In general, it is better to sit with your eyes closed (or half-closed, so that you don't fall asleep).

However, since such conditions are not always possible or convenient to you, much can still be accomplished by meditating while doing some other routine tasks, such as walking the dog, doing your laundry, or washing your dishes. We recommend five to twenty minutes of meditation, once or twice per day, depending upon your current level of stress. Meditation is not the core of this recovery program, but if you choose to meditate much more heavily than we have suggested, for any reason, it would be best to consult a meditation expert or master. Another caution is that people with seizure disorders should not meditate.

RELAXATION

An alternative to meditation is one of several physical relaxation techniques. The one we have found most effective and easily learned in our clinical practice is simply slow, deep breathing. Take a moderately deep breath in (don't strain). Then exhale very slowly. Repeat this as often as you need to until you feel sufficiently relaxed.

6. *Have fun. Reward yourself for recovery by seeking* natural *highs or ways of enjoying yourself.*

As we have pointed out before, all conditioning of behavior takes place by rewarding that behavior. Therefore, in order to build in new patterns of behavior, you will want to reward yourself for acting differently. Simply not drinking, gambling, overeating, or smoking, for example, is not a lot of fun! In order to give up those habits, it is far better that you replace them with other enjoyable activities. For example, you could plan to take your spouse to the movies for each week of abstinence, or to take a vacation in some exotic land in return for your own good behavior for set periods of time. Another example would be to buy yourself a gift that you could not have afforded had you been squandering your money on your habit of choice.

7. *Change people, places, and things as necessary in order to avoid excessive temptations.*

If you reliably get upset every time you see your mother-in-law, avoid seeing your mother-in-law. This makes sense, doesn't it? It also makes good sense to avoid the people who remind you of your addictive habit(s) or have the ability to trigger you into your older thought patterns. What if, every time you got high on cocaine, you did it in a yellow room? Is it not likely, then, that the color yellow might trigger you into craving cocaine? So avoid yellow rooms! If your habit of choice is horse racing, doesn't it make good sense to stay away from the track or your bookies' place of business? This is the kind of thinking we are talking about here. If you suspect or know for sure that some person, place, or thing reminds you of your addictive behavior of choice or of the positive feeling you used to obtain from it, then these are dangers to your abstinence and to your happiness. Avoid, avoid, avoid.

Remember, however, consistent with the ABC Theory, Bill Wilson said in *Alcoholics Anonymous*, "In our belief any scheme of combating alcoholism which proposes to shield the sick man from temptation is doomed to failure." In other words, it is not your exposure to triggers that causes your addictive behavior, but rather how you think about those triggers. By all means stay away from them as much as you can, especially in the early stages of recovery. But remember that you will never be entirely able to avoid exposure to those triggers. Therefore, your thinking had better be pretty clear. Bill Wilson calls this "being spiritually fit." He says that as long as you are spiritually fit, there is no reason to avoid tempting situations when you have a legitimate reason to be there. For example, there is no legitimate reason for an alcoholic to sit in a bar simply to watch a football game, but if he is thinking rationally, he should not have to avoid his daughter's wedding just because there will be champagne there. Similarly, we would certainly advise a cocaine addict not to hang around a crack-house for the sake of friend-ship or sex. But we would not tell him he has to quit his job because some coworkers use cocaine. There are some difficult situations that must be dealt with on an individual basis. One such example might be an obese chef. If that is his profession, it would be unreasonable to tell him to quit. However, in order for him to conquer his compulsive overeating, he might have to take some time off to get a start on his recovery. This is the kind of case where a professional therapist or counselor would be most useful even though no serious emotional disturbance may be involved.

8. *Use medications as prescribed by a psychiatrist or addictionologist.*

Medications might be prescribed to alleviate withdrawal symp-toms, reduce cravings or urges, and reduce anxiety and depres-sion upon making such tremendous changes in one's lifestyle. Sometimes, antidepressants and other psychiatric medications might be necessary to reduce the psychological problems that underlie a person's addictive behavior. This is too technical an area for this book to go into great detail about. In any case, sophisticated medical consultation is necessary to determine whether or not some medication or combination of medications are called for in your case.

9. *Don't use any addictive substances or engage in the addictive behav-iors of your choice.*

For any addictive chemical substances, as you know from the previous chapters, we recommend total abstinence. For some behavioral disorders such as compulsive sexuality or compulsive overeating, some compromises must be made. Many of the details have been dealt with in Chapter 14. Please read each section that mentions one of your problems even though it includes a problem you believe you do not have.

Remember, recovery involves the learning and reinforcement (rewarding) of new attitudes and behaviors. However, the old, established, addictive attitudes and behaviors still have permanent memory traces in your brain. Too often, exercising the very behavior that you are trying to recover from can reward the old learning and make it burst forth with equal or greater strength than your newly acquired behaviors. For example, it is usually a bad idea for the alcoholic to hang out at his favorite bar, drinking only orange juice, in order to socialize. It is usually a bad idea for the compulsive gambler to continue to hang out at the race track just to watch the horses without betting. This is because indulging in one link of the addictive chain of conditioned reactions stimulates the other links. This is what relapse is about.

10. *Keep it simple.*

In overcoming any irrational pattern of thinking, feeling, or behavior, it is important not to make things too complicated for yourself. For many years, AA has used a handful of slogans that help keep recovering people on track. We list some of them for you in the next section.

Jargon to Learn

"One day at a time"

This means that you can only live in the present, and that too much worrying about what is going to happen either tomorrow, or five or ten years from now, will not help you maintain your abstinence today. It seems to be a horrendous task to not drink (gamble, smoke, overshop, overeat, etc.) for the rest of your life. But, it seems a lot easier to abstain for just today, or maybe for just this next hour, or just the next twenty minutes, if necessary. So take your recovery one day at a time instead of seeing it as a lifelong burden.

"Turn it over"

The original AA meaning of this is to remind the recovering alcoholic of Step 3: Made a decision to turn our will and our lives over to the care of God *as we understood Him.*" For the Rational Emotive Behavior recovery program, the phrase is still appropriate to our version of Step 3, "I shall let rational thinking help me," which means little more than to stop demanding those things in life that you do not already have and are not likely to obtain.

In our clinical experience, most of the traditional twelve-steppers interpret the intended meaning of "Turn it over" as "Forget it." This interpretation closely applies to the Rational Emotive version of Step 3—accepting reality as it is rather than lamenting over how it should be but isn't.

"Take the cotton out of your ears and put it in your mouth"

This is a very different-sounding, but actually conceptually similar, interpretation of Step 3. It means "Learn to take advice." The humility of accepting the fact that none of us knows everything is not humiliating or shameful. We can all learn something, especially from others who have already taken the journey we wish to traverse. You can, too. The very nature of addiction supports and reinforces a kind of stubbornness of thinking that makes it difficult for the addict to hear the truth. Open-mindedness, which has been mentioned in previous chapters, is a necessity for recovery that cannot be overemphasized.

The Rational Emotive Behavior recovery program repeatedly admonishes you to take advice from those individuals whom you believe know more about something than you do. It also advises you to question and dispute your own fixed, rigid beliefs. Please remember that just because you believe something does not mean that it is true. Perhaps somebody else knows better than you do. That would not make you less of a person. It would simply prove that you are not omniscient, or all-knowing; *you* are not God.

"It works if you work it"

This statement is very clear. It simply means that if you follow the program, you will have a good chance at recovery. Thus, if you do not utilize the recovery program steps and do the exercises as we have prescribed, or follow the S.M.A.R.T program, or follow an SOS group, or follow the Gamblers Anonymous program, or follow the group geared to your addiction, what are your chances of recovery?

Most programs work if you follow their prescriptions *and believe* **fully** *in what you are doing while you are doing it.* Obviously, we recommend that you follow our Rational Emotive Behavior recovery program.

"Keep coming back"

Learning takes time. Do not feel like a failure if you have tried to give up one of your addictive habits and failed—even if you have failed several times. We have met many successfully recovering persons who have been through five, ten, or even fifteen programs before they finally gave up their self-defeating behavior and straightened out their act. You can do it, too! You can only do it if, instead of condemning yourself as a total failure, you keep returning to the work involved in the program.

Another, and very helpful and hopeful, interpretation is to keep returning (coming back) to the self-help group meetings. Don't label yourself as a failure or believe that you cannot recover simply because you have slipped or even relapsed. If at first you don't succeed, try, try again. Research and clinical experience shows that the more time spent in recovery attempts, the better the chances of full and lasting recovery.

Glossary of Recovery Terms

A—In REBT, **A** is the antecedent or activating event. It is what psychologists call the "stimulus," and what recovering people call the "trigger."

ABC Theory—In REBT, the theory states that it is not **A** (the stimulus) that causes **C** (the emotional and behavioral response), but rather **B** (the evaluative or judgmental belief about **A**) that is directly responsible for **C**.

ABCDE Method—In REBT, this is the self-help technique that teaches how to dispute and challenge the irrational beliefs (**B**'s) that cause inappropriate feelings and dysfunctional behaviors (**C**'s) using Rational Problem Analysis. Also see **D** and **E**.

Abstinence—In recovery programs, a total lack of indulgence in an addictive habit. In most cases, abstinence, rather than an attempt at controlled indulgence of the habit, is recommended.

Abuse—Any repeated indulgence in behaviors that are dangerous to yourself or others or have other serious consequences. The ability to stop the indulgence is present, and if it continues, it is completely voluntary. Continued abuse is often the first step in the development of an addiction, wherein control over the indulgence is lost. See also **dependence.**

Acceptance—In REBT and recovery programs, not demanding that reality be different from the way it is.

Addiction—Difficulty with voluntarily reducing or stopping one's indulgence in **abuse**. A significant sign of addiction is a lack of change in the indulgent behavior in spite of a self-demand to change the indulgence. Other signs are persistent desire and withdrawal effects when not actively indulging.

Amends—Attempts to right the wrongs that one has done to yourself and to others. These attempts can be direct or indirect (as explained in Chapter 9). Making amends helps clear the emotional baggage, such as guilt feelings, caused by the addictive behavior. This emotional baggage, as long as it lasts, has the potential to trigger relapse.

Awfulizing—In REBT, the act of taking a totally negative view of something that is only partially bad. This involves treating any real or conceptualized event as if it were a truly terrible catastrophe. See **catastrophizing**.

B—In the ABC Theory and the ABCDE Method, **B** is the belief about **A** that causes **C**. B is a judgmental or evaluative thought, opinion, or attitude. It can be rational, logical, and realistic, or it can be irrational, illogical, arbitrary, or unrealistic.

C—In the ABC Theory and the ABCDE Method, **C** is the emotional and behavioral results of believing **B** about **A**. When the evaluative, judgmental, attitudinal belief is irrational, the emotional response will be inappropriate, and the behavioral response will be dysfunctional.

Catastrophizing—The irrational belief (B) that something (A) that is somewhat negative is as bad as a true catastrophe. See **awfulizing.**

Chain of addictive conditioned reactions—A set of feelings and behaviors related to an addiction that follow each other chronologically, starting with a trigger and ending with indulging the addictive behavior and getting high from it. This chain is learned, or conditioned, and causes functional neurological connections (synapses) in the brain that are permanent in nature.

Cognitive Dissonance—The psychological conflict that arises when your behavior doesn't match your belief. Examples: taking a hit when you are thinking that you should be at a CA or NA meeting; going to an AA meeting when you are thinking that you need a drink.

Conditioning—Forms of learning that change an ordinarily neutral stimulus into one that causes a specific kind of emotional or behavioral reaction.

Cunning and baffling—A traditional twelve-step phrase referring to the difficulty of overcoming addictive indulgences.

Cure—Anything that completely eliminates a disease. While the tradition in twelve-step meetings refers to addiction as a disease, it is also traditional to teach that there is no cure for addiction. Therefore, all who stop indulging an addictive habit are said to be "in recovery" for the rest of their lives, or until they relapse.

D—In the ABCDE Method, **D** is rational disputing—questioning and challenging one's irrational beliefs. The goal is to rid oneself of irrational beliefs.

Demand—The irrational belief that something should or must be the way that you want it to be. Addicts characteristically are very demanding of life and of themselves. This tendency is called the **King Baby** attitude in traditional twelve-step programs. Its antidotes include humility and acceptance of reality on reality's terms.

Denial—In recovery programs, the refusal to accept the fact that you are addicted. This is part of the cunning and baffling nature of the disease.

Dependence—The inability to stop **abuse**, characterized by persistent desire and withdrawal symptoms. Also see **addiction**.

Discomfort anxiety—In REBT, an irrational fear and intolerance of any negative feelings. This is often an impetus for continuing addictive behavior and for maintaining a state of denial.

Dry drunk—In AA meetings, this refers to someone who is abstinent but not recovering and, therefore, is still acting like a drunk. For example, such a person may continue to show symptoms that were typical of his or her drinking days, such as dishonesty, argumentativeness, lack of concern for self and others, inappropriate spending, careless driving, and irresponsibility at work. The same syndrome also occurs when the habit of choice is other than alcohol. For example, the cocaine addict will still take unnecessary risks; the compulsive shopper may still watch the shopping networks on TV; the sex addict may still waste hours every day fantasizing about what he or she would *like* to be doing.

E—In the ABCDE Method, **E** is the emotional and behavioral effect of properly disputing irrational beliefs. The result is an appropriate emotional and behavioral response to whatever the activating event happened to be.

Empirical—Founded upon direct experience or observation of reality. This kind of thinking is the antidote to fantasies, illusions, and delusions caused by irrational demandingness, or by improper teaching.

Fake it 'till you make it—In traditional twelve-step programs, the idea of changing behavior on the basis of the idea that you know that it is better to act in a certain way even though you may not feel like acting that way. When you act against a current belief, you will usually feel like a fake, like you're acting. If you persist in acting in the way that you intellectually believe to be better, eventually your belief will likely become consistent with your behavior (see **cognitive dissonance**) and the feeling of being a fake will go away: you have then "made it."

Fuck it—Often the last thought by an addict prior to indulging, relapsing, or prior to indulging in addictive behavior in the face of the realization of long-range negative consequences. It really means "Fuck me."

God helps those who help themselves—In traditional twelve-step programs, this is the concept that the addict has to take personal responsibility for the recovery process, even though God will show him or her the way.

High—The feeling you get while, or immediately after, indulging an addictive habit. The feeling can also occur during anticipation of indulging.

Higher Power—The traditional twelve-step programs refer to this in terms of "God as you understand Him," and to spirituality. A broader definition would be anything that acts as a source of wisdom in helping the addict overcome the addiction.

Humiliation—Feelings of shame, embarrassment, and worthlessness, usually due to having your faults made public or known to others. It is caused by a lack of acceptance of your fallibility.

Humility—A recognition and acceptance of your fallibility, without undermining your self-esteem. The opposite of humiliation.

Impatience—Being unwilling to wait. This is an important component of **low frustration tolerance**.

Irrational—Illogical, unrealistic, absolutistic, demanding, awfulizing, or catastrophizing. Known in traditional self-help groups as **stinking thinking**.

It works if you work it—In traditional twelve-step programs, the implication that the program will always work if you would properly work the steps. That is, change only occurs if you take personal responsibility for changing your behavior.

King Baby—Frequently heard at "A" meetings, it refers to an atti-tude that promotes low frustration tolerance, such as, "I want what I want when I want it."

KISS—Keep it simple, stupid. Don't overcomplicate recovery by being overly theoretical—trying to understand the biochemistry of addiction, trying to solve deep theological problems, and so on—instead of moving forward in the program.

Logical—Using clear, correct, valid reasoning.

Long-range hedonism—Planning your activities in order to maxi-mize the total amount of lifelong pleasure or to minimize inter-fering with it.

Lost control—An inability to maintain moderate indulgence after you have become addicted.

Low frustration tolerance—The demand that reaching your goals, including feeling good, should be easy and not take much time or effort.

Musterbation—In REBT, another word for demandingness, espe-cially about your own behavior.

No pain, no gain—In REBT, as well as in traditional recovery pro-grams, this is the recognition that recovery is not easy, and that it can't always be comfortable.

One day at a time—In REBT as well as in the traditional twelve-step programs, advice to focus on the here and now instead of thinking about all of the discomfort and effort involved in life-long recovery.

People, places, and things—Refers to the triggers that, in the initial stages of recovery, should be avoided as much as possible, and later avoided unless there is some good reason to do otherwise.

Perfectionism—The belief that nothing should ever go wrong, and that people, especially yourself, should not have any faults. It is an especially self-defeating tendency if you happen to relapse, because it leads to feelings of hopelessness, which can mistakenly lead you to conclude that recovery is not possible.

Powerless—Often taken to mean that there is nothing that you can do about being addicted. See **lost control**, this program's replacement for this concept.

Rational—Logical, realistic, or scientific thinking and appropriate emotional and behavioral responses to such thinking. This kind of thinking is marked by an absence of unrealistic demandingness, absolutisms, overgeneralizations, and false dichotomies (I, you, he or she, or it am/is all good or all bad).

Rational problem analysis—See **ABCDE Method**.

Reality—That which is.

REBT—Rational Emotive Behavior Therapy. A form of cognitive-behavior therapy based upon the fact that your thinking, including beliefs, attitudes, judgments, evaluations, and opinions, strongly influence or directly cause your emotions and behaving. Thus, when your emotions and behaviors are unnecessarily self- or other-defeating, they can be changed by learning to think more rationally. See **ABC Theory** and **ABCDE Method**.

Recovery—The process of not indulging in destructive habits in spite of having become addicted. It has been discovered that recovery only occurs with rather far-reaching changes in your thinking, emoting, and behaving. Abstinence alone leaves you feeling deprived and always vulnerable to relapse. See **dry drunk**.

Relapse—Regularly indulging again after a period of abstinence, whether in recovery or not. See **recovery** and **slip**.

Rock bottom—Must be defined differently for different addictions. For chemical addictions, refers to inability to maintain a job and social relationships, heavy debts, medical problems, and the need to indulge just to get going in the morning. For gambling, health problems may not be an issue but the others are. For tobacco, the health issue is the major problem. For shopping, debt is the major problem. For sex, there are work, health, social, and financial problems that are paramount. For overeating, health problems are the major concern. For all of the addictions, guilt and low self-esteem is a major problem for those at, or on the way to hitting, rock bottom; thus, most people who are at rock bottom are clinically depressed and often suicidal.

Serenity Motto—See the Introduction for the quote of the motto. In this program, it is used for the same reason as the Serenity Prayer in traditional programs, but without reference to reliance on God. Instead, the motto emphasizes your internal motivations.

Serenity Prayer—See the Introduction for the quote of the prayer. It is used at all traditional Anonymous meetings. It is intended to remind people to maintain a sane outlook on life as they struggle with life's problems.

Setup—A plan to indulge in the addictive behavior, of which the addict, who is in denial, is unaware. That is, the chain of conditioned addictive reactions is unconsciously unfolding.

Short-range hedonism—The preference for immediate pleasure in spite of predictable, negative, long-term consequences.

Sick and tired of being sick and tired—A term frequently heard in traditional twelve-step meetings. The feeling the addict has who has hit **rock bottom.** This is often insincerely said by people who are seeking treatment but are not really ready to give up their addictive indulgences.

Slip—A single episode of return to indulgence that you stop by seeking help immediately, thus preventing a full-blown **relapse**.

Slip but don't fall—This cautions you not to turn a slip into relapse by deciding that you can't win over your addiction (i.e., that you are a total failure).

Spiritual—In traditional twelve-step program, the faith that a **Higher Power** will help the addict get through recovery. In this program, it refers to social connectedness. This can be an anti-dote to the social isolation that guilt, depression, and the indulgence itself often result in. Part of recovery is re-establishing normal social relationships instead of isolation, or only superficial relationships with other addicts or suppliers.

Sponsor—In traditional twelve-step programs, a person who is well into his or her recovery program and who volunteers to coach others attempting to stay in recovery, offering to be available at any time to help the sponsored person deal with urges to indulge.

Stinking thinking—In the traditional twelve-step programs, refers to irrational thinking that tends to lead to indulgence. See **irrational**.

Talking the talk—In traditional twelve-step programs, refers to those individuals who know the steps well enough to give advice to others and appear knowledgeable, but who do not themselves follow the program steps.

Trigger—A stimulus, whether internal to the addict's mind or something in the external environment (see **people, places, and things**), that initiates the chain of addictive conditioned reactions.

Turn it over—In the traditional twelve-step programs, is usually used to tell an addict who is upset or hurt to turn the matter over to a Higher Power. In other words, "forget it" or "let go of it." In this program the concept would refer to application of the ABCDE Method in order to help the person accept the reality of the upsetting factor.

Unmanageability—In the traditional twelve-step programs, the concept that the addict's life has been so disrupted by the addiction that it can no longer be handled without help from the program.

Urge—A desire or craving, sometimes physiologically determined, to indulge in the addictive behavior. It often serves as the trigger that initiates the chain of addictive conditioned reactions.

Walking the walk—In the traditional twelve-step programs, refers to those individuals who are genuinely applying the program to their personal lives. See **talking the talk.**

White-knuckling it—Refers to individuals who are trying to remain abstinent without changing themselves. In the traditional twelve-step programs it refers to those who are not trying to maintain conscious contact with their Higher Power. In this program, it more specifically refers to those who are not working at changing the way they think about reality.

References

Alcoholics Anonymous World Services. (1976). *Alcoholics Anonymous*. (3rd Ed.). New York: Alcoholics Anonymous World Services.

Cattell, R. B., Eber, H. W., and Tatsuoka, M. M. (1970). *Handbook for the 16 PF*. Champaign, IL: Institute for Personality and Ability Testing.

Cinciripini, P. M., Lapitsky, L., Seay, S., Wallfisch, A., Kitchens, K., and Van Vunakis, H. (1995). The effects of smoking schedules on cessation outcome: Can we improve on common methods of gradual and abrupt nicotine withdrawal? *Journal of Consulting and Clinical Psychology, 63*, 388–399.

Ellis, A. (1968). *RET in a Nutshell*. New York: Institute for Rational-Emotive Therapy.

Ellis, A. (1988). *How to Stubbornly Refuse to Make Yourself Miserable about Anything. Yes, Anything!* Secaucus, NJ: Lyle Stuart.

Ellis, A. (1994). *Reason and Emotion in Psychotherapy: Revised and Updated*. New York: Birch Lane Press.

Ellis, A. and Harper, R. (1975). *A New Guide to Rational Living*. North Hollywood, CA: Wilshire Book Co.

Ellis, A., McInerney, J. F., DiGiuseppe, R., Yeager, R. J. (1988). *Rational-Emotive Therapy with Alcoholics and Substance Abusers*. New York: Pergamon Press.

Ellis, A., and Velten, E. (1992). *Rational Steps to Quitting Alcohol.* New York: Barricade Books, Inc.

Hafner, J. (1981). *It's Not as Bad as You Think.* Center City, MN: Hazelden.

Krug, S. E. (1980). *Clinical Analysis Questionnaire Manual.* Champaign, IL: Institute for Personality and Ability Testing.

Peiser, K. (1992). *The ABC's of Emotions.* Chicago: PsychSoft Publishing.

Sandry, M. (1998). *Should I or Shouldn't I? Is That the Question?* Chicago: PsychSoft Publishing.

Trimpey, J. (1989). *Rational Recovery from Alcohol: The Small Book.* Lotus, CA: Lotus Press.

Index

KEN PEISER, PH.D. and MARTIN SANDRY, PH.D. have both maintained private practices in Rational Emotive Behavorial Therapy and have worked together for over thirty years on various clinical and writing projects. They are presently co-directors of Midwest Psychological Healthcare, P.C. and live in Chicago.